Zoroastrianism
The Divine Light
By Luiz Santos

Copyright © 2022 Luiz Santos
All rights reserved. No part of this book may be reproduced in any form or by any means without written permission from the copyright holder.
Cover image © Vellaz Studio
Review by Armando Vellaz
Graphic design by Amadeu Brumm
Layout by Matheus Costa
All rights reserved to:
Luiz A. Santos
Category: Zoroastrianism

Summary

Prologue 5
Chapter 1 The Foundations of Zoroastrianism 8
Chapter 2 The Divine Light 15
Chapter 3 Purification Rituals 22
Chapter 4 The Sacred Fire 29
Chapter 5 Truth (Asha) 36
Chapter 6 Angra Mainyu and Evil 43
Chapter 7 Amesha Spentas 51
Chapter 8 The Spiritual Journey 59
Chapter 9 The Practice of Charity 67
Chapter 10 Worship of Nature 75
Chapter 11 Cosmic Consciousness 83
Chapter 12 The Role of the Priests 91
Chapter 13 The Nowruz Ceremony 99
Chapter 14 The Importance of Prayers 106
Chapter 15 Spiritual Forces 114
Chapter 16 The Role of the Family 121
Chapter 17 Zoroastrian Ethics 129
Chapter 18 The Use of Mantras 136
Chapter 19 The Vision of Life After Death 143
Chapter 20 Spiritual Healing Techniques 151
Chapter 21 The Divine Nature of the Human Being 159
Chapter 22 The Covenant with Ahura Mazda 167
Chapter 23 Spiritual Renewal 174

Chapter 24 The Power of Offerings 181
Chapter 25 Rituals of Protection 188
Chapter 26 Dream Interpretation 195
Chapter 27 Paths to Wisdom... 202
Epilogue 210

Prologue

There is an ancient flame burning within the silent inner temple of every human being, an eternal fire that centuries have tried to extinguish but that rekindles, luminous, in every heart seeking truth. This flame, silent and immortal, calls you closer. In a world where darkness lurks in every corner, where anguish and fear try to infiltrate minds, this book reveals a different path: the path of light that inhabits your being, a light that has always been present and awaits the moment to emerge, radiant and complete. Each page will guide you, not with abstract ideas or empty concepts, but with a solid, ancient truth that unites the visible and the invisible, the human and the divine.

You are more than you think; in your essence, you carry the reflection of the light of Ahura Mazda, the symbol of order, wisdom, and clarity. This is not about beliefs or imposed dogmas but an invitation to reclaim your own nature, the one that pulses in harmony with the universe. The path awaiting you here is ancestral, traced millennia ago by those who heard the call of the spirit and rose up against the darkness spreading in their lives. These pages are not merely texts; they are a portal, a passage through which you enter a universe where each choice you make determines the expansion of light or the advance of shadows. Like the sacred fire in the oldest traditions, this work becomes the flame that burns, keeping chaos at bay and awakening the purest aspect of your soul.

Zoroastrianism, to which this book introduces you, is a path for those who aspire to renewal. And, contrary to what many might imagine, the battle between light and shadow is not confined to the cosmos; it reflects what happens within each individual. It is in your inner self that the forces of light and shadow face each other, where purity and corruption vie for territory with every thought, word, and gesture. You, the reader, are the protagonist of this epic, the guardian of a flame that burns beyond time and space. Every decision, every action aligned with the principle of asha—the universal order—becomes a manifestation of the eternal light that exists within you and all around you.

Prepare, then, to immerse yourself in purification rituals that go beyond the body, cleansing the mind and spirit from impurities accumulated through contact with the shadows of the world. By learning about the importance of water and fire, not as mere elements but as emanations of divine purity, you will be invited to rediscover these symbols as forces of transformation and protection. The sacred fire, kept alive in temples and in the hearts of the faithful, is the constant testimony of Ahura Mazda's presence, the reminder that light is inextinguishable and will always prevail over darkness.

Each word of this book is a spark that touches the flame burning within you. The practices, reflections, and teachings contained here are not a path outwards but a return to what has always been yours. The world around you—the movement of the stars, the fluidity of water, the warmth of fire—reflects the eternal dance between light and shadow, and you are called to partake in this movement, to balance in truth, to be one with asha. For those who dare to take this step, who accept this calling, a truth is revealed: chaos and destruction are ephemeral; light and order, eternal.

There is much more than a belief system in this work; what you will find here is a path of transformation, an invitation for your existence to become the very reflection of divine order. The daily practices, meditations, and rituals will guide you through a process of inner and outer purification, creating space for the divine to flow through every act and thought. You will then become a guardian of the light, someone who, with every step, challenges the power of the shadows and reaffirms the universe's purpose. What awaits you is the realization that true victory is achieved when the inner light aligns with the cosmic light, and that by honoring the purity of your spirit, you honor the purity of the entire universe.

The words of Zoroaster, the ancient prayers, and the sacred symbols you will encounter are not remnants of a distant past. They are keys, doors that open to a greater reality, timeless wisdom that remains alive for those who seek it. By the end of this book, you will realize that as you delve into the knowledge shared here, something within you has transformed, something that transcends the ordinary. You will be guided to understand that true enlightenment is not something acquired; it is a remembrance, a return to the original state of being, where light and order are inseparable from existence itself.

May this book become the fire that kindles your spirit, a flame that never fades. May you walk in asha, with peace in your heart and your spirit illuminated, as a true guardian of the light.

Chapter 1
The Foundations of Zoroastrianism

The origins of Zoroastrianism stretch back into the distant past, a path traced through time to ancient Persia, where the prophet Zoroaster—or Zarathustra—received his vision from the supreme being, Ahura Mazda. Amidst mountains and rivers, he experienced a revelation that would redefine the spiritual landscape of his people. Zoroastrianism, thus, emerged as one of the world's earliest monotheistic religions, weaving a tapestry of cosmic dualism, moral imperatives, and the promise of a world renewed by light.

Central to this vision is the eternal struggle between two forces: Ahura Mazda, the Wise Lord, representing order, truth, and light; and Angra Mainyu, the Destructive Spirit, embodying chaos, deceit, and darkness. This dichotomy is not merely a mythic struggle but a lens through which the adherents of Zoroastrianism view reality itself. Every action, thought, and choice becomes part of this cosmic battle, tilting the balance between the two. It is through the righteous path, known as asha, that one aligns with Ahura Mazda, embracing a life of integrity and purity.

The concept of asha is at the heart of Zoroastrian teachings—a principle that signifies truth, order, and the natural law governing the universe. It is the rhythm of life, the pulse that maintains the harmony between the heavens and the earthly realm. Through asha, the Zoroastrian perceives their role in sustaining the world's balance, choosing light over shadow in every aspect of existence. Living according to asha means embracing truthfulness in speech, justice in actions, and clarity of mind, thus fostering an inner environment where the Light Divine can flourish.

The presence of fire in Zoroastrian rituals is no mere coincidence. Fire, as a symbol, serves as the physical manifestation of the Light Divine—the essence of Ahura Mazda that permeates creation. In every temple, where sacred flames are maintained without interruption, one finds a reflection of the unending struggle to keep the darkness at bay. The faithful approach the fire with reverence, whispering ancient prayers that have crossed centuries. It is not the fire itself that they worship, but what it represents: the energy, purity, and brilliance of the Divine that constantly burns within and around us.

The prophet Zoroaster's teachings bring a profound simplicity to this cosmic framework, yet they do not shy away from the complexities of human existence. His vision, as enshrined in the Gathas—ancient hymns believed to have been composed by the prophet himself—conveys a message of hope, wisdom, and a call to humanity to awaken to its role as co-creators of the world's destiny. In these verses, he emphasizes the importance of choosing the righteous path, the path illuminated by the Light Divine, a path that promises the ultimate victory of good over evil.

But this journey toward the Light is not one of passive hope; it demands active participation. The individual is tasked with cultivating spenta mainyu, or a progressive mind, seeking knowledge, self-discipline, and compassion. Each person becomes a warrior in the fight against falsehood and injustice, a defender of the principles that uphold the order of the world. Here, Zoroastrianism lays a foundation that is both spiritual and ethical, where the divine and the earthly meet through the actions of each practitioner.

Zoroastrian cosmology presents a universe that is not merely a battleground but a living, dynamic space filled with the essence of asha and druj—truth and falsehood. The earth, the waters, the plants, and the very skies above are infused with this energy, and every aspect of the natural world participates in this ongoing dance between light and darkness. It is in this space that humanity finds its sacred duty: to protect and nurture life, to live in accordance with asha, and to ensure that the flames of the spirit burn brightly against the encroaching shadows.

The focus on purity in Zoroastrian practice is both literal and symbolic. Rituals of cleansing, prayers, and the maintenance of inner and outer sanctity are seen as acts of devotion to Ahura Mazda. Water, another symbol of purity, is revered alongside fire, used in rituals to purify the body and the soul. This spiritual hygiene extends to thoughts and actions, emphasizing a life lived with mindfulness and respect for the cosmic order. The clean, flowing waters and the bright, steady flame are reminders of the pure state that the soul strives to return to, beyond the physical constraints of the world.

Zoroastrianism's vision of the world, therefore, is deeply interconnected with the concept of the Light Divine. It is this light that gives life to the stars and sun, that dwells within the sacred fires, and that reflects the moral clarity that a true follower of Zaratustra aspires to achieve. The light is not distant; it is an ever-present guide, an inner flame that, when acknowledged and nurtured, leads to spiritual transformation. This light is the source from which all that is good and life-giving flows, and it is through the conscious choice to align with it that one draws nearer to the divine.

As Zoroastrians light their lamps and approach the holy flame, they are not merely performing an ancient custom; they are participating in an act that transcends time, echoing the primordial command to let there be light. The rituals and prayers that accompany this act are the keys that unlock a deeper connection to Ahura Mazda, the source of all wisdom and goodness. It is through these practices that one seeks to illuminate the inner temple, to become a reflection of the divine light, a vessel through which the eternal radiance can shine forth.

In the heart of these teachings lies the promise of a world renewed, where darkness retreats and the brilliance of asha is restored in its fullness. It is a hope that transcends individual salvation, envisioning a time when all creation will reflect the glory of Ahura Mazda, and the shadows cast by Angra Mainyu will be dispelled. Through the ancient words of Zoroaster, the Light Divine remains a beacon, a promise that as long as there are those willing to tend the flame, there is always the possibility of a brighter dawn.

The cosmology of Zoroastrianism unveils a complex tapestry, where every thread represents a delicate interplay between light and shadow, purity and corruption. Building upon the foundational ideas of Ahura Mazda and Angra Mainyu, this ancient faith explores the deeper mysteries of existence, the purpose of humanity, and the path toward spiritual elevation. Central to this vision are the Amesha Spentas—divine emanations or "Holy Immortals"—who serve as extensions of Ahura Mazda's will and guardians of the natural and spiritual realms.

Each Amesha Spenta embodies a unique aspect of creation, acting as both a protector and a guide. Vohu Manah (Good Mind) inspires wisdom and clarity, urging the practitioner to cultivate thoughts aligned with truth. Asha Vahishta (Best Truth) governs fire and order, upholding the cosmic law that ensures harmony. Khshathra Vairya (Desirable Dominion) offers strength and guardianship over the metals, symbolizing authority wielded with justice. Spenta Armaiti (Holy Devotion) watches over the earth, embodying love and devotion to the divine. Haurvatat (Wholeness) and Ameretat (Immortality) govern water and plants, respectively, representing the promise of spiritual completion and the eternal nature of the soul.

These seven divine beings, in their intricate roles, shape the spiritual journey of the faithful, guiding them through the material and immaterial worlds. The Amesha Spentas are not distant deities; they are the channels through which the Light Divine flows into the world, imbuing it with purpose and vitality. For the practitioner, seeking alignment with these divine forces is a crucial step toward achieving harmony within oneself and with the universe. Through prayer and ritual, one invokes their presence, seeking their aid in the ongoing struggle to embody asha and resist the seduction of druj, the forces of deceit and disorder.

Zoroastrian thought places great emphasis on the dual nature of humanity, reflecting the greater cosmic struggle. Each individual harbors both the potential for good and the susceptibility to darkness. This duality is not viewed as a flaw but as an opportunity—an arena where moral choices are made, and the inner battle between light and darkness unfolds. This understanding shapes the Zoroastrian's approach to life, where every decision, no matter how small, becomes a manifestation of either light or shadow. The essence of one's soul—fravashi—serves as a divine guide, whispering the truths of asha and urging the individual towards the path of righteousness.

The role of the fravashi, often described as a guardian spirit or higher self, is crucial in this spiritual framework. It is believed that each soul is accompanied by this divine essence, a fragment of Ahura Mazda's own wisdom, which strives to maintain the purity of its charge. The fravashi guides, but it does not impose; it is through the exercise of free will that each person must choose whether to heed this inner light or to follow the temptations of druj. Thus, Zoroastrianism places immense responsibility on the individual, emphasizing the active nature of spiritual growth.

The practice of self-reflection and meditation allows one to connect with this guiding spirit, fostering a deeper awareness of the thoughts and actions that align with asha. It is in moments of quiet contemplation, with the flickering flame of a candle as a companion, that the faithful seek clarity, listening for the subtle voice of the fravashi. These practices are not reserved for the elite but are seen as accessible paths for every believer to strengthen their connection to the divine, purifying the mind and the spirit.

The battle between light and darkness is also a reflection of the world's ongoing transformation. Zoroastrianism envisions a cosmic cycle where the forces of Angra Mainyu gradually weaken, as each soul that chooses the path of light contributes to the ultimate restoration of order. The final goal is Frashokereti, the renewal of the world—a time when all creation will be purified, darkness will be vanquished, and every soul will find its place in the perfected world. This is a vision not just of personal salvation but of universal redemption, a promise that the light will ultimately prevail.

In daily life, the struggle between light and darkness finds expression in the rituals and observances that shape the rhythm of a Zoroastrian's existence. The recitation of the Ashem Vohu and the Yatha Ahu Vairyo, two of the most sacred prayers, serves as both a reminder and an invocation of asha, reinforcing the connection between the individual and the divine order. These prayers, repeated at dawn, midday, and sunset, create a spiritual structure, aligning the practitioner's life with the cycles of nature and the movement of the stars—reflecting the belief that the cosmos and human actions are interwoven.

The discipline of prayer is further accompanied by acts of ritual purification. The Kushti, a sacred cord worn around the waist, symbolizes the commitment to the path of truth. Tied and untied during specific prayers, it is a constant reminder of the vows made to uphold asha. By wearing the Kushti, a Zoroastrian affirms their role as a protector of the light, an active participant in the world's renewal. This simple yet profound ritual connects the body, mind, and spirit to the greater struggle that defines the Zoroastrian way of life.

The physical world, in Zoroastrian belief, is not to be shunned or seen as illusory. Instead, it is a sacred space where the spiritual and the material coexist, where divine energy flows through the elements of fire, water, earth, and air. This belief transforms everyday interactions with nature into acts of reverence. A river becomes a manifestation of Haurvatat's wholeness, a tree an emblem of Ameretat's promise of eternal life. Caring for the environment is, therefore, not just an ethical choice but a spiritual duty, as it involves maintaining the purity that reflects Ahura Mazda's creative spirit.

In this light, the Zoroastrian path is one of active engagement with the world—a faith that finds the divine not in retreat from life but in the very act of living it fully, with integrity and awareness. By aligning with the principles of asha, the practitioner aids in the cosmic effort to bring forth the light, recognizing that each pure thought, each just action, contributes to the greater victory over chaos. This holistic vision encourages a balanced life, where spiritual growth and earthly responsibilities walk hand in hand, ever guided by the Light Divine.

Thus, the Zoroastrian worldview, with its intricate blend of cosmology and ethical practice, challenges each follower to see beyond the immediate and the mundane, to glimpse the eternal battle playing out in every corner of existence. It is a faith that invites the seeker to embrace the light within, to recognize the divine presence in the world's wonders, and to take their place as a guardian of asha in an ever-unfolding story of creation and renewal. The journey of the Zoroastrian is one that constantly strives for purity, knowing that through their devotion, the light within and the light of the universe can become one.

Chapter 2
The Divine Light

Within the sacred teachings of Zoroastrianism lies a profound reverence for the concept of the Divine Light, an essence that flows from Ahura Mazda and permeates every corner of the cosmos. This Light is not merely a physical radiance, but a spiritual force that sustains life, shapes existence, and offers a direct channel to the highest wisdom. To understand the Divine Light is to glimpse the very heart of Zoroastrian thought—a luminous thread that binds together creation, the human soul, and the eternal struggle between order and chaos.

The Divine Light is considered the purest expression of Ahura Mazda's presence, an extension of His creative energy. It is both the source and the destination, the beginning that holds the promise of a renewed world and the guiding force that leads the faithful through the shadows. This Light manifests in many forms, from the glow of the sun that gives life to the earth to the sacred fires kept alive in Zoroastrian temples. Each spark, each flickering flame, becomes a reminder of the unyielding presence of Ahura Mazda, a visible link between the earthly realm and the divine.

In Zoroastrian cosmology, the Divine Light is the primal element that gave birth to the universe, a radiant burst that pushed back the darkness and shaped the cosmos. It is through this light that the world gained its form, and every creature came to embody a spark of its brilliance. Even amidst the constant opposition of Angra Mainyu, the Destructive Spirit, this light persists, ever-present, illuminating the path of those who choose to walk in truth and righteousness. It is the presence that whispers hope even when night seems darkest, promising the renewal that follows every cycle of shadow and light.

Meditation on the Divine Light becomes a key practice for Zoroastrians, a way to deepen their connection with Ahura Mazda's energy. Unlike ritualized prayer, this meditation is a quiet, inward journey, seeking to visualize and align with the Light that resides within. It begins with focusing on a single flame, watching as it dances and pulses, symbolizing the eternal flame that burns in the spiritual realm. As the practitioner sinks into contemplation, they imagine the light expanding, filling their body, their mind, and eventually the space around them. It is an act of opening oneself to the flow of divine energy, allowing the self to become a vessel through which the Light Divine might manifest.

This practice is not merely about achieving a peaceful state of mind; it is a spiritual discipline aimed at awakening the khvarenah, a term that Zoroastrians use to describe the divine glory or spiritual radiance that each person carries within. The khvarenah is akin to a protective aura, a shield forged from the light of Ahura Mazda that repels darkness and nourishes the spirit. When one meditates on the Divine Light, they are, in essence, seeking to strengthen their khvarenah, to make it shine brighter, and to align their personal glow with the greater radiance of the cosmos.

The importance of light is also seen in the symbolism of fire in Zoroastrian ritual. The sacred flame, burning within the fire temples, is not just a physical object; it is a living, breathing presence. To stand before the fire, to offer prayers and invocations, is to come face to face with a manifestation of the Divine Light itself. The fire is both witness and participant, consuming the offerings and returning them to the spiritual realm. It is a bridge, allowing communication between the material and the immaterial, the seen and the unseen.

In the quiet moments of dawn or the deep stillness of night, when a Zoroastrian lights a small candle or gazes into the temple fire, they are reminded of their place in this cosmic design.

The act is simple, yet profound, reflecting the belief that the Divine Light is ever-reaching, seeking to touch every soul, to guide it back toward the eternal source. For those who meditate upon this light, it becomes a reminder that even in the darkest moments, there is a spark within that can never be extinguished.

This intimate relationship with the Divine Light extends to the Zoroastrian understanding of the sun and stars. To observe the sun rising each day is to witness the triumph of light over darkness, a daily reminder of Ahura Mazda's enduring presence. The stars, in their silent vigil over the night, are seen as beacons of spiritual power, guiding souls through the mysteries of existence. The faithful see in them the watchful eyes of the Amesha Spentas, the holy beings who accompany Ahura Mazda in the care of the world, casting their light upon those who seek truth.

Yet, the connection with the Divine Light is not confined to solitary moments or ritual observances. It is meant to permeate every aspect of life, guiding thoughts, words, and actions. To live in the Light is to act with kindness, to speak with honesty, and to strive for a purity of spirit that reflects the clarity of a flame untainted by smoke. In this way, the Divine Light becomes a practical guide, shaping ethical behavior and encouraging a life lived in service to others. It inspires the faithful to see beyond the mundane and to recognize the sacred in every interaction.

In essence, the Divine Light is a call to transcend the ordinary and to aspire toward the spiritual potential that lies within every human heart. It is a reminder that each choice, no matter how small, can either dim or brighten the inner flame. To align oneself with this light is to step into a larger story, a cosmic dance where every action contributes to the victory of asha over druj, order over chaos.

The vision of the Divine Light also carries with it a promise—a promise that at the end of all struggles, at the conclusion of every journey, there is a place of pure, unblemished radiance where the faithful will find rest. This promise is not just for the individual soul but for all creation, for the earth itself, as it moves toward Frashokereti, the ultimate renewal. It is a vision of a world where the barriers between the divine and the material dissolve, where every being reflects the unending brilliance of Ahura Mazda.

Thus, the Divine Light is both a guide and a goal, an ever-present reminder of the sacredness that underlies all life. Through meditation, through prayer, and through daily acts of devotion, the Zoroastrian draws closer to this light, ever seeking to become a clearer, purer vessel through which it might shine. The journey is demanding, requiring both discipline and an open heart, but it is a path that leads, inexorably, toward the dawn that will one day illuminate all things.

To delve deeper into the Divine Light is to embrace practices that bring this radiant essence into daily life, transforming meditation into a lived experience. The Zoroastrian tradition provides a series of time-honored exercises—meditative, visual, and breath-based—that allow one to feel the presence of this energy, to channel it, and to use it as a force for both spiritual growth and protection. These practices are more than rituals; they are pathways, guiding the seeker toward a direct and intimate communion with the essence of Ahura Mazda.

One of the foundational practices involves the visualization of light. This begins with a simple act—closing one's eyes, breathing deeply, and envisioning a small flame flickering within the heart. As each breath is taken, the flame grows stronger, its warmth spreading throughout the chest, filling the practitioner with a sense of peace and clarity. This light, imagined first as a spark, soon expands beyond the physical body, enveloping the practitioner in a sphere of radiant, golden light. This is the Light Divine, a protective and purifying aura that shields the soul from negativity and draws it closer to the cosmic presence of Ahura Mazda.

In these moments, the seeker is encouraged to focus on the qualities of the light—its warmth, its purity, and its infinite nature. With each exhale, one releases tension, darkness, and impurity, letting them dissolve into the light that surrounds them.

This breathing technique, known as Nehvar, combines visualization with rhythmic breathing, creating a harmony between body, mind, and spirit. It is said that through such practices, one not only feels the Divine Light but begins to radiate it outward, becoming a beacon for others in times of darkness.

Another core exercise involves the use of mantras, ancient Zoroastrian chants that act as keys to unlock deeper states of consciousness. The Ashem Vohu—"Righteousness is the best good, it is radiant and it is bliss"—is a mantra often used during meditations on the light. When recited with intention, it vibrates through the body, resonating with the very essence of asha, the cosmic order. This chant, repeated softly or within the mind, is imagined as a current of light flowing through the practitioner, cleansing away impurities and aligning the inner self with the universal rhythm.

The use of light in physical spaces is another aspect of this connection. Zoroastrians often maintain a sacred flame within their homes, a candle or a small oil lamp that burns as a symbol of their devotion. Lighting this flame is more than a ceremonial act—it is an invitation for the Divine Light to enter the home, purifying the space and creating a sanctuary against negative influences. As the flame burns, practitioners may offer prayers or simply sit in silent contemplation, allowing the light of the fire to merge with the light they hold within.

These practices also extend to the creation of a protective shield, a ritual for times when one faces spiritual challenges or feels the weight of negative energies. In this exercise, the practitioner stands before the sacred flame, focusing intently on its steady glow. With deliberate breaths, they visualize the light growing, forming a sphere that encircles their body. This sphere is imagined as a translucent, impenetrable barrier, infused with the energy of Ahura Mazda, capable of repelling any darkness that seeks to encroach upon it.

The practitioner then walks through their home or sacred space, holding this vision, allowing the sphere of light to extend and embrace every corner. Each step is taken with a silent prayer, asking the Divine Light to cleanse and protect the space. This act is not only a defense but a reaffirmation of the Zoroastrian's role as a guardian of the light, a reminder that the forces of asha stand ready to aid those who choose to uphold its principles. It transforms everyday living into a sacred practice, where even the act of maintaining one's space becomes a spiritual duty.

For those who wish to deepen their daily engagement with the Divine Light, the morning ritual of facing the sun is particularly profound. At dawn, the practitioner stands beneath the open sky, eyes closed, and lifts their face toward the rising sun. This moment of greeting the day is filled with intention, as they visualize the rays of the sun merging with their inner light, expanding it, empowering it. The warmth of the sun becomes a reminder of Ahura Mazda's presence, a daily renewal of the connection to the source of all creation. It is believed that in these moments, one can almost hear the whispers of the cosmos, a quiet assurance that the struggles of the world are but shadows cast by the brilliance of the light.

This practice, known as Khorshed Yazata, is more than a physical act; it is a spiritual alignment, a way of positioning oneself as a participant in the eternal cycle of light overcoming darkness. It calls upon the presence of the Divine Light to fill the heart with courage and the mind with clarity, making each new day an opportunity to bring asha into the world. In times of hardship, these moments by the sun serve as a reminder that even when the night seems endless, the dawn is always near.

Integrating these practices into a daily routine gradually transforms the practitioner's perspective, allowing them to perceive the world through the lens of the Divine Light. Obstacles become challenges to be met with resilience, relationships become opportunities to share kindness and compassion, and solitude becomes a space for reflection and inner illumination. It is a path that encourages an awareness of the subtle energies that flow through all things, a deeper understanding of how every thought, every breath, and every action contributes to the greater harmony of the cosmos.

Yet, the journey with the Divine Light is also a deeply personal one. Each practitioner, as they explore these practices, finds their own way of connecting to the light, of making it a living presence in their lives. Some may feel it most strongly in the silence of meditation, while others may discover it in the shared warmth of community prayers or the quiet glow of a candle in the night. This flexibility is at the heart of Zoroastrian spirituality, where the rituals provide a structure, but the true transformation comes from the individual's open-hearted engagement with the sacred.

As one continues along this path, the presence of the Divine Light becomes more than a concept—it becomes a companion, a guiding star in the journey toward Frashokereti, the renewal of all things. The practices taught by Zoroaster, and carried through the centuries by the faithful, serve as a map for this journey, guiding the seeker back to the source, where all shadows dissolve and only the radiant truth of Ahura Mazda remains. Through these daily acts of devotion, one learns that the Light Divine is not distant, but ever near, ready to embrace all who reach out to it with sincerity and hope.

Chapter 3
Purification Rituals

Purification holds a place of deep significance within Zoroastrianism, acting as the bridge between the mundane and the sacred. The process of cleansing the body, mind, and spirit is not just a preparation for prayer or ritual but a fundamental aspect of aligning oneself with the principles of asha—the cosmic order. Through these purification rituals, practitioners seek to create a vessel that is worthy of the Divine Light, a space where the presence of Ahura Mazda can dwell without obstruction.

Among the most revered elements in these rituals are fire and water, each serving a dual role as both physical and spiritual purifiers. Fire, as the visible embodiment of the Divine Light, burns away impurities, transforming the physical into the ethereal, the material into the spiritual. Its warmth is a reminder of Ahura Mazda's presence, a constant companion that protects and guides. In temples, the sacred flame is never extinguished, a living symbol of purity and continuity, but in the home, even a small candle becomes a tool for connection.

To approach the fire in prayer, one must first be cleansed, respecting the sanctity of the element. This often involves the use of ab-zor—pure water, believed to carry a divine essence that can wash away the physical and spiritual stains gathered from the world. The act of washing the hands and face with this blessed water is more than a practical gesture; it is a symbolic renewal, a shedding of the burdens that may cloud the spirit. This ritual, called Padyab, is typically performed before any prayer or act of devotion, ensuring that the body and mind are in harmony with the pure energies of the fire.

Water itself, revered in rivers, springs, and even in the droplets used for rituals, represents the flow of life and the continuity of asha throughout creation. In Zoroastrian tradition, bodies of water are seen as under the protection of the Yazata (divine spirit) Haurvatat, the guardian of wholeness. To stand by a river, to feel its cool touch, is to commune with this divine presence, to open oneself to the currents that carry both physical sustenance and spiritual rejuvenation. Many practitioners find a profound sense of peace and clarity when performing ablutions in natural water sources, especially during the early morning when the sun, another source of divine energy, casts its first light over the earth.

A key ritual that embodies the principles of purification is the Kushti, the untying and retying of the sacred cord. The Kushti is a thin belt made of woven lamb's wool, wrapped three times around the waist and tied with special knots. It symbolizes the commitment to a life of purity and truth, and the act of untying it signifies a moment of introspection—a brief pause in which the practitioner releases the impurities of thoughts and actions accumulated since the last prayer. Re-tying the Kushti is an affirmation, a declaration of intent to continue walking the path of asha, embodying righteousness and clarity.

The Kushti ritual is typically performed alongside the recitation of the Ashem Vohu and Yatha Ahu Vairyo prayers, sacred verses that resonate with the frequencies of cosmic order and the victory of light over darkness. These prayers not only purify the space around the practitioner but also reinforce the inner alignment with the Divine Light. To perform this act is to stand in a space where the personal and the cosmic meet, a reminder that each individual is a microcosm, a reflection of the universe's greater struggle and harmony.

Zoroastrians also practice rituals involving the use of gaomez, a substance made from the urine of a specially prepared bull, which is believed to have purifying properties. Although this element may seem unusual from an outside perspective, it holds deep symbolic value. It represents the physical aspect of purification, an offering from a consecrated animal, symbolizing the removal of druj—the energies of falsehood and chaos—from the physical environment. Sprinkled around homes or sacred spaces, it serves as a protective barrier, ensuring that the domain remains aligned with the energies of light and truth.

These purification practices are not just for the individual; they extend to the community as well. Collective rituals often take place around a consecrated fire, where the gathered faithful join in prayer, purifying not only themselves but the very air they breathe. The smoke from the sacred fire rises, carrying the intentions and prayers upward, connecting the earthly with the celestial. It is believed that in such moments, the boundaries between the human and the divine thin, allowing the energy of Ahura Mazda to flow freely among those gathered.

The purity of thought is another crucial aspect in Zoroastrian purification rituals. It is understood that the mind must be kept clear, free of envy, hatred, or deceit, as these emotions can obscure the light within. To harbor negative thoughts is to allow Angra Mainyu, the spirit of darkness, a foothold in one's heart. Therefore, purification rituals often begin with a period of quiet reflection, allowing the practitioner to recognize and release these negative emotions before proceeding with their prayers or rites. This internal cleansing is as vital as the washing of hands or the donning of the Kushti, for it prepares the soul to be receptive to the blessings of the Divine Light.

Moreover, these rituals emphasize the importance of keeping one's environment clean and ordered, a reflection of the cosmic order that Zoroastrians strive to maintain. The home, like the body, is seen as a microcosm of the universe. Just as the soul must be purified, so too must the spaces one inhabits. Sweeping away dust, washing floors, and keeping windows open for sunlight to enter are acts that mirror the spiritual process of removing impurities from the self. This attention to physical cleanliness creates a space where the energies of light can dwell, making the home a place where prayer and connection to Ahura Mazda feel natural and undisturbed.

Purification rituals are not solely about maintaining distance from impurity, but about actively inviting the energies of life and renewal into one's existence. They remind the practitioner that purity is not a state to be achieved once, but a process—an ongoing commitment to cultivating a life that reflects the order, truth, and radiance of the divine. Through these rituals, the Zoroastrian builds a life that is constantly in dialogue with the higher realms, where each act of purification is a step toward deeper understanding and alignment with the cosmic dance of light.

To stand before the fire, having completed the rites of purification, is to be ready—ready to receive, ready to offer, and ready to become a vessel through which the Divine Light might flow. It is a moment of humility, where the individual acknowledges their place within the grand scheme of creation, yet it is also a moment of profound strength, for they carry within them the power of a light that no darkness can extinguish. Through the daily discipline of purification, the Zoroastrian prepares not just for the challenges of the world but for the inner journey toward the ultimate promise of renewal and transformation.

The journey into the depths of Zoroastrian purification rituals reveals a world where every gesture, every breath, and every thought is interwoven with the sacred. These practices are designed not only to cleanse but to transform the practitioner, aligning them more closely with the rhythms of asha. The rituals unfold like a series of steps, each one building upon the last, creating a pathway toward a deeper, more profound connection with the Divine Light.

One of the most essential of these rituals is the Kushti, the sacred cord ritual, which goes beyond a simple act of purification—it is a declaration of intent to live a life devoted to asha. To perform the Kushti properly, one begins by finding a quiet space, free from distractions, ideally facing a source of natural light like the morning sun or the sacred flame. The practitioner unties the Kushti from around their waist while reciting the Kem Na Mazda, a prayer of protection, acknowledging Ahura Mazda as the shield against the darkness of Angra Mainyu.

As the Kushti is untied, the practitioner holds it in their hands, allowing a moment of silence to reflect on any negative thoughts or actions they wish to release. They breathe deeply, envisioning the darkness dissolving into the light around them, letting go of impurities that have accumulated in both body and spirit. Then, while reciting the Ashem Vohu, they begin to wrap the Kushti around their waist again, winding it three times to symbolize the three core tenets of the faith: good thoughts, good words, and good deeds. The tying of each knot is accompanied by a prayer, sealing their commitment to walk the path of asha.

The repetition of this ritual throughout the day, at dawn, midday, and sunset, serves as a reminder that purification is a continual process. It brings the mind back to the essence of Ahura Mazda's teachings, reinforcing the alignment with the divine with each knot and every whispered prayer. It is a practice that keeps the light close, ensuring that no matter how the darkness might press in, the soul remains steadfast in its clarity and purpose.

The Padyab—the washing ritual with ab-zor, or blessed water—complements the Kushti by preparing the body and mind for prayer and ritual. To perform this ritual, the practitioner begins by cupping water in their hands, lifting it toward the light, and offering a quiet blessing. This act transforms the water into a conduit for divine energy. They then wash their face, hands, and feet, all the while focusing on the cleansing nature of the water, imagining it as liquid light that flows through them, washing away both physical and spiritual impurities.

The environment where these rituals are performed is crucial, for the space itself should mirror the purity sought within. Before beginning, the area is cleansed through the sprinkling of ab-zor or by wafting the smoke from sacred herbs like sandalwood or frankincense. These elements, chosen for their purifying properties, fill the air with a fragrance that is said to repel negative energies, creating an atmosphere where the connection to the Divine Light can flow unimpeded. Incense is lit in the four corners of the space, a tribute to the elements and the divine guardians that watch over each direction, asking for their protection and presence.

The rituals involving the sacred fire are perhaps the most intricate and central to the Zoroastrian practice of purification. To prepare for a fire ritual, practitioners gather wood that has been blessed and dried, offering it to the flame with prayers of gratitude. The fire is kindled carefully, ensuring that it burns cleanly, without smoke—symbolizing a life lived without the cloud of deceit or anger. As the flames grow, the practitioner offers libations of hom juice (a sacred extract) or sandalwood to the fire, murmuring prayers like the Atash Niyayesh, which praises the fire as a messenger of Ahura Mazda, a bridge between the seen and unseen realms.

During the ritual, the practitioner stands before the fire, reciting ancient verses from the Yasna, focusing on the heat and light of the flames, imagining them as the very breath of Ahura Mazda. The warmth from the fire is felt as a physical manifestation of the Divine Light, purging the inner shadows and filling the heart with the courage to face the battles of daily life. It is said that through these moments, one can hear the quiet crackle of the wood as the whispers of asha, a soft, ever-present reminder that the light will always triumph over darkness.

For those seeking a more immersive experience, the practice of Zarathushtra's Ab-Zor—a ritual purification bath—offers a powerful way to connect to the energy of water as a source of divine renewal. This ritual is performed near a flowing stream or, in modern adaptations, within the privacy of a home. The water is blessed with prayers invoking Haurvatat, the Yazata of wholeness, and the practitioner steps into it with a prayer on their lips, imagining the water washing over them as a river of light. The ritual is both an act of humility and a recognition of the sacredness of the natural world, reinforcing the bond between the practitioner and the elements.

These rituals serve as practical tools for maintaining a spiritual balance but are also invitations to deeper states of contemplation. Through the repetitive, rhythmic nature of these acts, the mind enters a meditative state, opening itself to the subtle messages of the spirit. It is within this space that the most profound transformations occur—where the boundaries between the practitioner's light and the greater Light Divine blur, and the sense of separation between self and cosmos fades.

The effect of these rituals extends beyond the moments in which they are performed. A home that has been ritually cleansed, a body that is regularly purified, becomes a vessel that radiates light into the world, affecting the space and people around it. It is not uncommon for Zoroastrians to bless the doorways and windows of their homes, asking for the protection of the Divine Light and marking these entryways with small symbols of asha, such as stars or flames, drawn with ab-zor. These symbols serve as reminders that the sacred is always near, that every threshold crossed is a step into the presence of the divine.

For those who undertake these practices, the sense of renewal and alignment is palpable. They come to understand that purification is not about attaining an impossible ideal of perfection, but about returning, time and again, to the source of purity within and beyond. It is a reminder that, despite the challenges and imperfections of human life, the opportunity for renewal is ever-present, as constant as the flow of a river or the steady burn of a flame.

The Zoroastrian way of purification thus creates a rhythm, a dance between the elements of fire and water, between the body and the spirit. Each ritual is a note in a larger symphony of devotion, played in harmony with the pulse of the universe. To participate in this dance is to feel oneself becoming a living expression of the light, a bearer of the ancient promise that the darkness shall not endure. Through these practices, the faithful learn that purity is not a state to be held but a path to be walked, where every step is a return to the light, and every breath is a prayer to the eternal flame that burns within.

Chapter 4
The Sacred Fire

The presence of fire within Zoroastrianism is more than a symbol; it is the manifestation of the Divine Light on earth, a tangible bridge between the physical world and the spiritual realm. In the flickering flames of the sacred fires, the faithful see the embodiment of Ahura Mazda's purity, an unbroken connection to the eternal.

The centrality of fire in Zoroastrianism is deeply rooted in the teachings of Zoroaster himself. In the ancient hymns of the Gathas, fire is revered as a symbol of asha, the cosmic order that sustains life and balances the universe. It is believed that when Zoroaster received his divine revelations, he understood that fire was not to be worshipped as a deity, but as a sacred witness to the divine truth. To stand before the fire is to stand before a living presence that reflects the light of Ahura Mazda, purifying the mind and spirit through its unwavering glow.

In the temples dedicated to Zoroastrian worship, known as Atash Behrams or Fire Temples, the sacred flame is treated with utmost reverence. It is kept burning continuously, never allowed to diminish or extinguish. This eternal flame represents the constancy of Ahura Mazda's light, a reminder that even amidst the cycles of time and the shifts between day and night, the divine presence remains unchanged. The fire is fed with sandalwood and other fragrant woods, each offering a gift to the divine, carrying prayers upward in spirals of smoke that mingle with the invisible world.

Zoroastrian tradition recognizes different grades of fire, each with its own level of sanctity and purpose. The Atash

Behram, the highest grade, requires a complex consecration process involving the purification and merging of sixteen different fires, each collected from a variety of sources such as the hearth of a home, a lightning strike, or a craftsman's forge. This process, which can take months, symbolizes the gathering of diverse elements of life into a unified, purified whole. When completed, the Atash Behram becomes a focal point for the community's spiritual life, a place where the divine and the earthly meet.

In addition to the Atash Behram, there are Atash Adarans and Atash Dadgahs, which serve as places for more localized worship and daily prayers. These fires, though of lesser ritual complexity, still hold profound importance. They are the centers around which the community gathers to offer their daily prayers, seek guidance, and renew their connection to the divine. Each time a practitioner steps into a fire temple, they are reminded of their role as a caretaker of this light, one who ensures that it continues to shine against the darkness of Angra Mainyu.

The rituals surrounding the sacred fire are precise, emphasizing the importance of purity. Those who tend the flame, known as Mobeds (priests), must maintain a state of ritual cleanliness, wearing masks to prevent their breath from contaminating the sacred element. The fire itself is treated as a living being, one that requires care, respect, and devotion. This deep respect is reflected in the way Zoroastrians approach the fire, with bowed heads and quiet prayers, recognizing that they stand in the presence of a profound mystery.

Beyond the confines of the temples, fire also plays a central role in the lives of Zoroastrians at home. Each household is encouraged to light a small flame daily, a reminder of the eternal light that guides their path. This simple act, performed in the morning or evening, becomes a moment of connection with Ahura Mazda. As the flame flickers, the faithful may recite the Atash Niyayesh, a prayer that praises the fire as a pure, luminous force that stands as a guardian against the darkness. It is a prayer of gratitude and humility, acknowledging the role of the fire as a keeper of spiritual clarity.

The significance of fire extends beyond prayer to moments of life's transition—birth, marriage, and even death. Fire is present at every stage, from the consecration of a marriage through the light of a sacred lamp, to the tending of the Atash Dadgah during funerary rites, guiding the soul through the realms of transition. For the Zoroastrian, fire is a constant companion, a guide that illuminates the path from this life to the next, ensuring that the soul remains aligned with asha even as it journeys beyond the physical world.

Yet, the meaning of the sacred fire also reaches into the philosophical heart of Zoroastrianism. It symbolizes the inner fire of the soul, the khvarenah—the divine glory that each individual carries within. Just as the temple flames must be fed and tended, so too must the spiritual flame within each person be nurtured. This inner light, when cultivated through prayer, meditation, and acts of righteousness, becomes a source of protection and guidance, allowing the individual to become a radiant presence in the world. It is through this inner fire that the faithful find the strength to face challenges, to resist the allure of falsehood, and to shine forth with the clarity of truth.

The relationship between the physical fire and the inner fire is seen as deeply intertwined. The warmth of the flames that a Zoroastrian tends within their home or temple becomes a reflection of the warmth they cultivate within their heart. It is a reminder that, in a world where darkness and chaos are always seeking to spread, the presence of even a single light can change everything. To keep the fire is to keep hope alive, to be a guardian of a promise that stretches back to the dawn of creation.

The sacred fire, in all its forms, thus serves as a beacon, a focal point that calls the faithful back to their purpose. It is a reminder that life itself is a kind of offering, one that must be given with sincerity and devotion. Through the daily act of tending the fire, Zoroastrians reaffirm their commitment to asha, ensuring that they remain aligned with the cosmic order that flows from Ahura Mazda's light.

In a world that often feels uncertain, where shadows seem to lengthen with each passing day, the sacred fire stands as a testament to endurance, to the belief that light will always have the power to overcome. For the Zoroastrian, to tend the flame is to participate in the ongoing story of creation, to become a co-creator with the divine, ensuring that the light of truth, purity, and compassion continues to burn brightly in a world that so desperately needs it.

Creating and maintaining a sacred fire at home is an act that transforms ordinary space into a sanctuary, inviting the presence of Ahura Mazda's divine essence. For Zoroastrians, the fire is more than a symbol—it is a living link to the spiritual realm.

The process of creating a sacred fire begins with the preparation of the space. It is essential to choose a quiet and clean area within the home, ideally a place where natural light can enter, yet remains sheltered from wind and disturbance. The space should be purified before the fire is lit, using water blessed with the recitation of the Ashem Vohu and Yatha Ahu Vairyo prayers. The practitioner sprinkles the water around the area, visualizing it as liquid light that drives away any lingering shadows, making the space receptive to the presence of the sacred flame.

Once the space is prepared, gathering the right materials becomes the next step. Traditional Zoroastrian practice calls for using dried sandalwood and fragrant herbs, such as frankincense or myrrh, which are believed to carry purifying properties. These materials are chosen not only for their ability to produce a steady, clean flame but also for their symbolism. Sandalwood represents the resilience and constancy of the Divine Light, while the aromatic smoke that rises from burning herbs is seen as a physical offering, carrying the practitioner's prayers into the spiritual realms.

With the materials ready, the act of kindling the fire itself is done with deep reverence. The practitioner lights the fire using a clean flame, reciting a prayer of invitation, calling upon Ahura Mazda to bless the fire and the space it inhabits. One common invocation during this process is the Atash Niyayesh, a prayer that honors the fire as a pure element and a visible sign of divine grace. The prayer is spoken slowly, with each word treated as a breath that feeds the flame, imbuing it with sacred intention.

As the fire begins to burn, the practitioner offers small pieces of sandalwood to the flames, allowing the wood to catch and feed the fire's life. Each offering is made with a silent intention, a moment of connection between the physical and the divine. The practitioner may recite short verses of the Yasna, the ancient liturgy, to deepen the atmosphere of reverence and to align their inner light with the outer flame. In these moments, the fire becomes more than a natural phenomenon; it is a presence that listens and responds, a companion in the spiritual journey.

Maintaining the purity of the sacred fire is crucial. The fire must be tended regularly, ensuring that it burns cleanly and is never allowed to die out suddenly, as this is believed to disrupt the flow of divine energy. If the fire must be extinguished, it is done so gently, with the remaining ashes collected and placed in a sacred or natural space, such as the base of a tree or into running water, as a way of returning the purified matter to the earth. These ashes, touched by the sacred flame, are seen as blessed and can be used to mark the doorway of the home or to consecrate other objects and spaces.

The daily maintenance of the fire involves a quiet ritual of rekindling, performed ideally at dawn and dusk. These times are considered liminal, moments when the boundaries between the physical world and the spiritual are at their thinnest. As the fire is revived, the practitioner takes time to reflect on their actions, thoughts, and prayers of the day, offering any burdens or concerns to the flame, allowing them to be consumed and transformed into light. This practice creates a rhythm that centers the day around moments of reflection and renewal, ensuring that the connection to the Divine Light remains strong and vibrant.

A key aspect of using the sacred fire as a channel for divine connection involves the practice of Mithra, the cultivation of silent, heartfelt communication with the divine. Sitting before the sacred fire, the practitioner quiets their thoughts, focusing on the gentle crackle of the wood and the warmth that radiates from the flames. They envision the fire not just as a source of heat but as a mirror of the inner spiritual fire, reflecting back the purity and clarity of the soul. In this state of meditation, the practitioner speaks to Ahura Mazda or listens for the subtle guidance that arises from the heart, allowing the fire to act as a mediator between their innermost self and the cosmic order.

The sacred fire also plays a central role in communal rituals, even when practiced within the home. Family members may gather around the flame for prayers, using the fire as a focal point for shared devotion. During festivals such as Nowruz, the Zoroastrian New Year, the fire is decorated with offerings of flowers and fruits, and special invocations are made to bless the coming year with light and prosperity. The fire becomes a source of unity, drawing together individuals in a shared commitment to upholding asha in their lives.

The act of offering to the fire is not limited to physical materials like wood or incense. Intentions, wishes, and prayers are often symbolically "placed" into the flames, allowing them to be carried upward as the smoke rises. In times of personal struggle or spiritual challenge, practitioners may write down their concerns on small pieces of paper, offering them to the fire with a prayer for guidance or release. The act of watching the paper burn, seeing the flames transform worries into ash, can be profoundly cathartic, reminding the practitioner of the impermanence of troubles and the enduring nature of the light.

Maintaining the purity of the fire also involves mindfulness in its presence. One does not speak harshly or act with anger before the sacred flame, as such behaviors are believed to disturb the harmony of the space. Instead, the fire invites a spirit of calm, of gentle contemplation, and of the pursuit of wisdom. It becomes a place where the practitioner is reminded to bring forth their highest self, to align their thoughts and actions with the path of asha.

The benefits of these practices are manifold. Over time, the presence of the sacred fire in the home becomes a source of strength and protection, its energy warding off negative influences and creating an atmosphere that fosters spiritual growth. It is said that the light of the sacred fire, once kindled and nurtured, begins to permeate the home, filling each room with a sense of peace and vitality. This radiance extends beyond the home, touching the lives of all who come into contact with it, reminding them of the presence of the divine in the everyday.

In maintaining the sacred fire, the Zoroastrian participates in a lineage of devotion that stretches back through centuries, becoming a guardian of a tradition that has withstood the tests of time. The fire represents the continuity of faith, the promise that no matter the challenges faced, the light of Ahura Mazda will continue to burn within the hearts of those who seek it. Through these practices, the home becomes a temple, and the flame a constant reminder that each life, no matter how small, can become a vessel for the Light Divine, shining brightly amidst the shadows of the world.

Chapter 5
Truth (Asha)

At the heart of Zoroastrianism lies the profound concept of asha, a term that encompasses truth, order, and the underlying cosmic law that governs the universe. Asha is not merely a moral guideline; it is the very structure of reality, a force that upholds the harmony between all elements of creation. It represents the divine order established by Ahura Mazda, and to live in accordance with asha is to align oneself with the natural rhythm of the cosmos, becoming a participant in the eternal flow of light that opposes chaos and deceit.

Zoroaster, through his divine revelations, presented asha as the pathway toward a life of purity, both physical and spiritual. In his hymns, the Gathas, he speaks of asha as the path to righteousness, the guiding star that leads the faithful away from the darkness of druj—falsehood, chaos, and evil. This duality, the opposition between asha and druj, is fundamental to the Zoroastrian understanding of the world. It is the lens through which the battles of life, both internal and external, are understood.

To follow asha is to make a conscious choice to pursue truth in thought, word, and deed—an idea encapsulated in the Zoroastrian triad: Humata (Good Thoughts), Hukhta (Good Words), and Hvarshta (Good Deeds). These principles form the basis of a life aligned with asha, urging the practitioner to cultivate a mind that is clear and focused on the good, to speak with honesty and kindness, and to act with integrity and compassion. Each aspect of this triad is seen as a thread that, when woven together, creates a life that reflects the divine order.

Living in alignment with asha means recognizing that every action has a resonance, a ripple that extends beyond the self, influencing the balance of light and darkness in the world. It is the understanding that by choosing truth and righteousness, one strengthens the very fabric of the universe, contributing to the victory of light over the darkness embodied by Angra Mainyu. This understanding places immense responsibility on the individual, as each moment becomes an opportunity to affirm or weaken the presence of asha in the world.

The pursuit of asha is also deeply personal, as it involves a continuous journey of self-reflection and moral clarity. For the Zoroastrian, this means examining one's own thoughts and actions daily, asking whether they align with the principles of truth. It is a practice that fosters humility, acknowledging that the path of asha is not always easy to discern, and that mistakes are a part of the human experience. Yet, each mistake is seen as an opportunity for growth, a chance to learn and realign with the divine order.

The principle of asha extends beyond human actions to encompass the entire universe. The stars that move across the sky, the changing of the seasons, and the cycles of birth and death are all seen as expressions of asha. Ahura Mazda, as the source of this cosmic order, is the eternal guardian of asha, ensuring that even when the forces of druj appear to gain strength, the balance of creation remains intact. This belief offers a sense of hope and stability, a reminder that beneath the apparent chaos of life, there is a deeper order that remains unbroken.

In practical terms, the teachings of asha guide the Zoroastrian's approach to ethics and relationships with others. It emphasizes justice, fairness, and the importance of fulfilling one's duties with sincerity. To be true to asha means to honor one's commitments, to act with integrity even when faced with difficulty, and to uphold the dignity of all beings. This extends to the way one treats the natural world, with respect and care, recognizing that the earth, waters, and all living things are part of the divine order that asha seeks to protect.

Yasna 30, one of the central hymns in the Gathas, describes asha as the guiding principle that leads to the "better path," urging humanity to choose wisdom over ignorance, light over darkness. In this verse, Zoroaster calls upon his followers to align themselves with asha, warning that the choice between following asha or druj shapes not only their own destiny but the fate of the world. This choice is presented as an ongoing struggle, a daily battle within the soul of each person, where every thought, word, and action tips the balance toward order or chaos.

One of the ways Zoroastrians actively engage with asha is through their prayers and daily meditations. The recitation of the Ashem Vohu—"Truth is the best good; it is radiant, it is bliss"—is central to this practice. Each recitation is more than a ritualistic act; it is a reaffirmation of commitment to living a life in alignment with asha. As the words flow from the lips of the faithful, they are meant to resonate within the mind and heart, reminding the practitioner of their role as a guardian of truth and a participant in the cosmic order.

In moments of moral dilemma or confusion, Zoroastrians are encouraged to pause and meditate upon the light of asha. This involves visualizing the light as a beacon, cutting through the fog of uncertainty, revealing the path that aligns with the highest good. This practice is both a spiritual and practical tool, aiding in decision-making and fostering a sense of inner peace, knowing that each choice, when made in alignment with asha, contributes to the greater harmony of the universe.

The impact of asha extends into the communal life of Zoroastrians as well. Communities are built around the shared values of truth, justice, and mutual respect, with each member striving to support the others in their pursuit of a righteous life. This collective commitment to asha creates an environment where the light is more vibrant, where the struggles of the individual are met with the strength and support of the community. Temples, gatherings, and family prayers all serve as spaces where the presence of asha is celebrated and renewed.

Ultimately, asha is a call to a deeper awareness—a realization that the world is not simply a stage for personal gain, but a sacred space where every being has a role to play in maintaining the balance between light and darkness. The Zoroastrian way of life, with its emphasis on purity, truth, and devotion, is an invitation to see beyond the material and to recognize the hidden currents of the divine that shape existence. Through the practice of asha, one learns to view each day as a new opportunity to be a channel for the light, to reflect the brilliance of Ahura Mazda in all that they do.

In embracing asha, the Zoroastrian does not seek to escape the world but to transform it, to bring forth the latent order that lies beneath the surface of everyday life. They see in the flow of the river, in the warmth of the sun, and in the flicker of a candle, the ever-present rhythm of asha, guiding them toward a future where the light will ultimately overcome all shadows. To follow this path is to join in the eternal work of creation, to add one's voice to the ancient hymns that sing of a universe where truth, beauty, and goodness reign supreme.

To embody asha is to transform everyday life into a continuous practice of aligning with cosmic truth and order. The principles of Zoroastrianism encourage each practitioner to integrate asha into their thoughts, words, and actions, making it a living force that guides decisions and interactions.

The first step in embodying asha lies in the cultivation of Humata, or good thoughts. Zoroastrians are taught that the mind is the origin of all actions, and as such, it must be kept clear, focused, and aligned with the principles of asha. A simple but powerful meditative exercise is to sit quietly in the presence of a flame, focusing on the steady glow as a representation of the mind's potential for clarity. The practitioner observes their thoughts as they arise, allowing them to come and go like the gentle flickering of the flame, without clinging to negative patterns or judgments. This practice, known as Atash Bandagi, encourages the mind to become like the fire—pure, unclouded, and steadfast in its devotion to light.

During this meditation, the practitioner may recite the Ashem Vohu prayer softly, letting each word echo within the mind. The prayer acts as a reminder that truth is not an abstract ideal but a lived reality that can be reflected in every thought. As the mind settles into a rhythm of calm, the practitioner imagines the light of the flame spreading through their thoughts, burning away any shadows of doubt, anger, or envy. This visualization transforms the mind into a space where asha can dwell, allowing the practitioner to emerge from the meditation with a sense of renewed focus and inner peace.

Beyond meditation, asha also guides how one speaks and interacts with others, encapsulated in the principle of Hukhta, or good words. Words carry energy, and in Zoroastrianism, they are considered as acts that shape the world around them. To speak truthfully and with kindness is to align with asha, while words spoken with malice or falsehood invite the chaos of druj. Practitioners are encouraged to adopt the habit of mindful speech, taking a moment before speaking to ensure that their words reflect their inner commitment to truth and righteousness.

A practical exercise for fostering Hukhta involves daily reflection at the end of each day. The practitioner may sit before a small fire or candle, allowing its light to illuminate their thoughts as they consider the words they have spoken throughout the day. They reflect on moments where they spoke with honesty and clarity, as well as those where their words may have been hasty or unkind. This process is not one of self-reproach but of gentle correction, a chance to offer up any errors to the fire and to vow to align more closely with asha in the future. This ritual of reflection strengthens the habit of conscious speech, ensuring that the practitioner's voice becomes a source of light in the world.

The third aspect of embodying asha is Hvarshta, or good deeds. Zoroastrians are called to transform their inner devotion into tangible actions that uphold justice, protect the vulnerable, and care for the earth. The practice of charity and service to others is seen as a direct expression of asha, where the individual becomes a channel through which Ahura Mazda's light can reach those in need. This service is not limited to grand gestures; it is found in the small acts of kindness that shape daily life, from offering a meal to a neighbor to helping maintain the cleanliness of public spaces.

One way to integrate Hvarshta into daily life is through the practice of Zand Yasht, a ritual of offering and gratitude performed at the beginning or end of each day. The practitioner places a small offering—such as a few grains of rice or drops of sacred water—into the fire, accompanied by a prayer of thanks for the opportunities to serve and for the strength to continue following the path of asha. This offering symbolizes a commitment to act with integrity and compassion, recognizing that each action, however small, contributes to the greater balance of light and darkness in the world.

Incorporating asha into the physical environment is another important aspect of daily practice. Zoroastrian teachings emphasize the purity of space as a reflection of the purity of the spirit. Keeping one's home clean and orderly is seen as an act of devotion to asha, a way of creating a space where the divine light can dwell. Practitioners are encouraged to keep a small flame or lamp burning in a dedicated area of the home, treating it as a focal point for prayer and reflection. The presence of this flame acts as a reminder that the commitment to asha must be maintained in both the inner and outer aspects of life.

For those seeking to deepen their connection to asha, the use of specific prayers and invocations can be a powerful aid. The Yasna 12, a hymn dedicated to truth and righteousness, serves as a profound meditation on the nature of asha. Reciting this hymn before the sacred fire, the practitioner is reminded of their role in the cosmic struggle between light and darkness, drawing strength from the words that have been chanted by countless generations before them. The verses call upon Ahura Mazda and the Amesha Spentas, invoking their guidance and protection in the quest for truth.

This practice can be combined with the ancient ritual of Nehvar, where the practitioner sits with their hands cupped around the flame, focusing their breath in a rhythmic pattern that matches the rise and fall of the light. As they breathe in, they imagine drawing in the purity of asha; as they exhale, they release any lingering doubts or impurities, offering them to the flame. This practice fosters a deep sense of unity with the divine, helping the practitioner feel the flow of asha through their own body and spirit.

The communal aspects of asha are equally important. In Zoroastrian communities, the commitment to asha is reinforced through shared rituals and ceremonies, where the faithful gather to renew their vows to truth and to support one another in their spiritual journey. Community members are encouraged to resolve disputes with fairness, to offer help where it is needed, and to create a culture where honesty is valued above all else. These gatherings are opportunities to reflect together on the teachings of Zoroaster and to strengthen the bonds of trust and compassion that asha requires.

By following the path of asha, Zoroastrians believe they contribute not only to their own spiritual growth but to the cosmic balance that sustains the world. Each act of truth, each kind word, and each moment of mindful thought is seen as a small light that joins the greater illumination of Ahura Mazda's presence. This understanding transforms daily life into a spiritual practice, where the boundaries between prayer and action dissolve, and where the sacred is found in the simple acts of living with integrity.

In embracing asha, the practitioner becomes a guardian of a tradition that sees the potential for divine light in every corner of existence. They learn to look at the world through a lens of wonder and respect, recognizing the interconnectedness of all things and the role of each being in maintaining the balance of creation. Through the teachings of asha, the Zoroastrian way of life offers a path where the pursuit of truth becomes a journey of deep inner transformation, guiding the soul toward the promise of renewal that lies at the heart of the divine order.

Chapter 6
Angra Mainyu and Evil

In the vast expanse of Zoroastrian cosmology, the presence of darkness is embodied in the figure of Angra Mainyu—also known as Ahriman—the Destructive Spirit. As the antithesis of Ahura Mazda's creative and life-giving force, Angra Mainyu represents the essence of druj, a term that signifies falsehood, chaos, and corruption. This malevolent spirit is the source of all suffering and evil in the world, standing in direct opposition to asha, the cosmic order and truth. To understand Angra Mainyu is to confront the nature of evil itself, recognizing its power and influence while also learning how to resist and overcome it.

Zoroastrian teachings describe Angra Mainyu as a being of pure negativity, whose very existence seeks to disrupt the harmony that Ahura Mazda has woven into the universe. Unlike the Divine Light, which nurtures and sustains, Angra Mainyu's nature is to divide, to distort, and to lead souls away from their true purpose. He is not simply an adversary in the abstract but a force that actively opposes every manifestation of asha, seeking to sow disorder in the hearts of men and in the fabric of the world.

This struggle between Ahura Mazda and Angra Mainyu is not viewed as a battle between equals. Zoroastrianism holds that ultimately, Ahura Mazda's wisdom and light are supreme, destined to bring about the final victory in Frashokereti, the renewal of the world. However, within the current state of existence, Angra Mainyu's influence is potent, and the conflict between these two forces plays out in every corner of the cosmos—most profoundly within the hearts of individuals. It is within this internal battlefield that the Zoroastrian faces their most significant trials, as they strive to choose asha over druj in their thoughts, words, and actions.

Angra Mainyu's influence manifests through a myriad of temptations and distortions that seek to lure individuals away from their higher nature. These temptations are not only physical but also deeply psychological, targeting the mind's inclination toward doubt, fear, and resentment. Negative emotions such as anger, jealousy, and hatred are seen as shadows cast by Angra Mainyu, obscuring the light of khvarenah—the divine radiance that each soul carries. When a person gives in to these darker impulses, they create space within themselves for druj to take root, weakening their connection to asha and the Divine Light.

In the Zoroastrian view, Angra Mainyu's influence is also evident in the natural world through decay, disease, and death. These are seen as disruptions to the natural harmony that Ahura Mazda intended for creation, signs of the corruption that Angra Mainyu brings into the material plane. Yet, even in the face of these adversities, the faithful are taught to respond not with despair but with a commitment to restoring balance. By nurturing life, healing, and cultivating purity, they oppose Angra Mainyu's intentions, reaffirming their role as protectors of the cosmic order.

A crucial aspect of the Zoroastrian understanding of evil is that it thrives on the absence of light and clarity. Angra Mainyu's power is not inherent but parasitic, feeding on ignorance and spiritual negligence. This is why vigilance is emphasized in Zoroastrian practice—remaining mindful of one's thoughts and actions is seen as a form of spiritual defense, a way of preventing the shadows of druj from encroaching upon the mind. It is said that the light of a single candle can dispel darkness in a room, and so too can the light of a single good thought weaken the grip of evil over the soul.

The teachings of Zoroaster stress that the struggle against Angra Mainyu is both individual and collective. Each person's effort to resist druj contributes to the broader battle for the soul of the world. This collective aspect is seen in rituals of community prayer and in the gathering of Zoroastrians to renew their vows to asha. When the faithful come together to recite the Ahuna Vairya—a powerful invocation that calls for the triumph of order over chaos—they are not only strengthening their personal resolve but also sending a wave of spiritual light into the world, weakening the influence of Angra Mainyu.

The Ahuna Vairya, a central prayer in the Zoroastrian liturgy, is particularly significant in this battle against darkness. It is believed that Zoroaster himself received this prayer from Ahura Mazda as a weapon against Angra Mainyu. Reciting this prayer is said to invoke the protective presence of the divine, creating a barrier against the forces of corruption. When spoken with deep concentration, the words of the Ahuna Vairya vibrate with the energy of asha, driving back the shadows and fortifying the soul against the encroachments of evil.

In addition to prayer, the presence of fire plays a protective role in warding off the influence of Angra Mainyu. The sacred flames, maintained in temples and homes, serve as more than symbols of the Divine Light; they are spiritual fortresses. Zoroastrians believe that Angra Mainyu cannot endure the presence of purity, especially in the form of fire, which represents the undiluted essence of asha. This belief leads to the practice of lighting candles or lamps during times of trial or uncertainty, inviting the power of the flame to dispel any lingering negativity.

Beyond the rituals and prayers, Zoroastrians are also taught practical ways to combat the influence of Angra Mainyu through acts of kindness, charity, and justice. By bringing goodness into the world, they weaken the foothold that druj has in their communities. The act of helping those in need, providing comfort to the suffering, and upholding truth in difficult situations becomes a direct means of resisting the spread of darkness. Each good deed is viewed as a strike against Angra Mainyu's dominion, a way of expanding the reach of asha in the world.

Zoroastrian teachings also recognize the importance of mental resilience in this struggle. Practitioners are encouraged to cultivate an inner strength that allows them to face challenges without succumbing to despair or cynicism. This strength is born from the knowledge that while Angra Mainyu's influence is real, it is also temporary. The soul that remains steadfast in its commitment to asha can weather even the darkest storms, emerging with a deeper connection to the light of Ahura Mazda. This resilience is seen as a reflection of the eternal nature of asha itself—a force that, no matter how much it is challenged, endures.

Angra Mainyu's presence in the world is thus a reminder of the stakes involved in the human journey. It calls for vigilance, but it also highlights the potential for heroism in every soul. The struggle against evil is not merely a burden; it is an opportunity for growth, for deepening one's understanding of the Divine Light and for playing a role in the cosmic story of creation's renewal. Each moment of choice, each act of kindness, and each recitation of a prayer is a small but meaningful step in this larger battle, contributing to the eventual victory of asha.

Through these teachings, Zoroastrianism offers a framework for understanding and confronting the presence of suffering and evil in the world. It acknowledges the reality of Angra Mainyu's influence without succumbing to fear, focusing instead on the power of the light that every individual carries within. By embracing this light and allowing it to guide their actions, Zoroastrians participate in the ancient struggle that Zoroaster first spoke of—ensuring that no matter how strong the darkness may seem, it is ultimately the light of asha that will shape the destiny of the world.

The battle against Angra Mainyu, the Destructive Spirit, is one that extends beyond the realm of concepts—it requires active, practical engagement through spiritual disciplines, prayers, and the cultivation of inner strength. Zoroastrianism provides its followers with specific methods and rituals to shield themselves from the influence of druj and to strengthen their connection with the Divine Light.

One of the primary tools for protection in the Zoroastrian tradition is the recitation of the Ahuna Vairya, a prayer that serves as a spiritual shield. This prayer is believed to have been revealed to Zoroaster by Ahura Mazda as a powerful weapon against Angra Mainyu. Its words resonate with the force of asha, and when recited with deep focus and intention, it is said to create a barrier of light that repels the darkness. Practitioners are encouraged to recite the Ahuna Vairya at key moments throughout the day—upon waking, before sleep, and whenever they feel the presence of negative thoughts or energies encroaching.

To maximize the effectiveness of the Ahuna Vairya, it is often combined with a visualization technique where the practitioner imagines a sphere of light expanding around them as they chant. This sphere grows brighter with each repetition, forming a protective layer that surrounds their body and mind. As the light expands, it pushes away shadows and obscurities, creating a sanctuary of calm and clarity. This visualization is not merely an exercise of imagination; it is believed to engage the divine energy that flows through the universe, making the practitioner's space a place where Angra Mainyu's influence cannot easily penetrate.

Another powerful practice for resisting the influence of Angra Mainyu is the ritual of Sagdid, which focuses on purifying spaces and banishing negative energies. Traditionally performed during funerary rites to protect the souls of the deceased from the corruption of druj, Sagdid can also be adapted as a home purification ritual. For this, practitioners place a burning piece of frankincense or sandalwood on a charcoal disk, allowing the purifying smoke to fill each room of the home. As they move through the space, they recite verses from the Yashts—hymns dedicated to the divine spirits who guard the natural order—asking for their protection and the dispersal of any lingering darkness.

While Sagdid is a ritual of external cleansing, Zoroastrian teachings also emphasize the importance of internal purification to combat the influence of Angra Mainyu. This begins with maintaining a disciplined practice of Padyab, or ritual washing. Before engaging in prayer or meditation, the practitioner washes their face and hands with ab-zor, blessed water that symbolizes the cleansing power of truth. As the water flows over the skin, they visualize it washing away the subtle influences of druj, renewing their spirit for the battles of the day.

Additionally, the wearing of the Kushti, the sacred cord, serves as a constant reminder of the commitment to truth and purity. The knots of the Kushti represent the eternal struggle between asha and druj, and the act of tying and untying them throughout the day reinforces the practitioner's vow to resist the temptations of Angra Mainyu. As the Kushti is wrapped around the waist during prayer, the practitioner recites the Kem Na Mazda, a prayer that asks for Ahura Mazda's protection against the forces of deception and corruption. This prayer, repeated at dawn, noon, and dusk, aligns the wearer's thoughts and actions with the Divine Light, creating a rhythm that integrates spiritual awareness into the fabric of daily life.

For moments of intense spiritual challenge or when faced with feelings of doubt, fear, or anger—emotions that Zoroastrians believe are stirred by Angra Mainyu—meditative practices like Atash Bandagi become crucial. In this meditation, the practitioner sits before a fire or candle, focusing on the steady, unwavering flame. They breathe deeply, drawing in the warmth and purity of the fire, and imagine it merging with their own inner light, strengthening their khvarenah and dispelling shadows from the heart and mind. This meditation serves as a direct way to reconnect with the essence of asha, allowing the fire to burn away impurities and restore a sense of balance.

Prayers to the Yazatas—divine spirits who assist Ahura Mazda in maintaining cosmic order—are also a key part of Zoroastrian spiritual defense. Invoking the protection of these beings, such as Mithra, the guardian of truth and contracts, or Sraosha, the spirit of obedience and divine listening, helps fortify the practitioner's resolve. Specific prayers like the Mithra Yasht or the Sraosha Yasht are recited to invoke their presence, asking for guidance and strength in moments when the influence of druj feels overwhelming. These prayers are often accompanied by offerings of fragrant woods or libations of pure water, gestures that reinforce the connection between the practitioner and the divine guardians.

The power of communal practice should not be underestimated in the struggle against Angra Mainyu. Gatherings at the fire temple, where the community comes together to pray before the sacred flame, create a collective force of spiritual light that repels darkness. The shared recitation of the Ahuna Vairya and Ashem Vohu prayers amplifies their power, weaving a network of light that binds each individual to the greater struggle for truth. These communal prayers remind practitioners that they do not face the challenges of druj alone; they are part of a lineage that stretches back to Zoroaster himself, united in their dedication to the path of light.

Furthermore, the practice of charity (Dāna) is seen as a practical way to weaken Angra Mainyu's hold on the world. By engaging in acts of service, helping those who are suffering, and giving freely without expectation of return, Zoroastrians enact the principles of asha and directly counter the selfishness and division that druj seeks to spread. The simple act of providing food to the hungry or shelter to those in need is seen as a blow against Angra Mainyu, a tangible way to transform the world into a place where the light can shine more brightly.

Zoroastrians are also encouraged to keep a journal of their spiritual struggles, recording moments when they feel the presence of druj in their thoughts or actions and how they responded. This practice, known as Ravaet, involves writing down prayers and reflections, turning the pages of the journal into a record of victories over negativity and a source of strength for future challenges. Reading through these entries serves as a reminder of the progress made on the spiritual path, providing encouragement during difficult times and a sense of continuity in the ongoing battle against darkness.

Ultimately, these rituals and practices are not just defenses against external threats but tools for inner transformation. They teach the practitioner to recognize the presence of darkness not as an insurmountable enemy but as a challenge that strengthens their devotion to asha. The struggle against Angra Mainyu becomes a path of growth, leading to a deeper understanding of the self and the divine. It is through this struggle that the soul is refined, becoming a clearer vessel for the light that Ahura Mazda wishes to pour into the world.

In this way, Zoroastrianism offers a dynamic approach to the challenges of life, one where the presence of evil is not denied, but faced with the full power of ritual, prayer, and compassionate action. The tools provided by Zoroaster and his teachings serve as a map, guiding each practitioner through the shadowed valleys of existence with the promise that, at the end of all struggles, the light will prevail. Through their daily efforts, Zoroastrians become bearers of this promise, keeping alive the hope that the world can be renewed, that asha will triumph, and that the flames of truth will continue to burn bright, no matter how dark the night may seem.

Chapter 7
Amesha Spentas

The Amesha Spentas, or "Bounteous Immortals," are central to the cosmology of Zoroastrianism, serving as divine emanations of Ahura Mazda. They are not deities in themselves, but rather aspects of Ahura Mazda's boundless nature, each representing fundamental principles that govern the universe and guide the spiritual journey of every Zoroastrian. Understanding their roles and qualities is crucial for those who seek to align with the divine order of asha and draw closer to the essence of the Divine Light.

The concept of the Amesha Spentas is rooted in Zoroaster's revelations, where he described these spirits as both guardians of creation and guides for humanity. Each of the seven Amesha Spentas embodies a particular virtue, and together, they represent the complete manifestation of Ahura Mazda's creative power. They act as intermediaries between the supreme deity and the physical world, each one overseeing a specific aspect of creation and offering spiritual protection and guidance to those who invoke their presence.

The most prominent of these is Spenta Mainyu, often translated as the "Holy Spirit" or "Beneficent Spirit." Spenta Mainyu represents the creative force of Ahura Mazda, the energy that opposes the destructive tendencies of Angra Mainyu. It is through Spenta Mainyu that the Divine Light flows into the world, nurturing growth and fostering life. In human terms, Spenta Mainyu encourages the cultivation of positive thoughts, actions, and intentions, guiding practitioners toward a life in harmony with asha. It is seen as the spirit that directly inspires individuals to seek truth, wisdom, and the betterment of themselves and others.

Vohu Manah, or "Good Mind," is another key Amesha Spenta, representing the principle of divine wisdom and the capacity for good thoughts. Vohu Manah is considered the bridge between the human mind and the divine consciousness, helping to elevate the thoughts of those who seek to understand the deeper mysteries of existence. Zoroastrians believe that invoking Vohu Manah aids in overcoming confusion and ignorance, opening the mind to the clarity of asha. This spirit is often invoked during moments of decision-making, when clarity and understanding are needed to choose the path that aligns with the greater good.

Armaiti, or "Devotion" (sometimes referred to as "Holy Harmony"), embodies the principles of love, patience, and humble service to the divine. Armaiti is the guiding force behind acts of compassion and selflessness, encouraging practitioners to live in a way that supports the well-being of others and the harmony of the natural world. She is considered the guardian of the earth, representing the sacred relationship between humanity and nature. Through Armaiti, Zoroastrians are reminded that true devotion is expressed not only through prayer but also through the care and respect given to the living world around them.

Kshathra Vairya, often translated as "Desirable Dominion" or "Divine Power," represents the ideal of just rule and the use of strength for the protection of the weak and the preservation of order. Kshathra Vairya embodies the principle that power should be exercised with wisdom and compassion, never with tyranny or cruelty. This spirit is often associated with the metal sky and the strength of the elements, symbolizing resilience and the ability to withstand challenges. Zoroastrians invoke Kshathra Vairya when seeking to strengthen their willpower and to act with courage in the face of adversity, upholding the principles of asha even when it is difficult.

Haurvatat, meaning "Wholeness" or "Perfection," and Ameretat, meaning "Immortality," are closely linked and represent the divine gifts of health, completeness, and eternal life.

Haurvatat is associated with the element of water, symbolizing the nurturing and healing aspects of existence, as well as the flow of spiritual wisdom. Zoroastrians turn to Haurvatat for strength in times of physical or emotional healing, seeking the balance that brings peace and well-being. Ameretat, on the other hand, is associated with the eternal nature of the soul, representing the promise of spiritual immortality and the continuation of life beyond physical death. Together, Haurvatat and Ameretat remind practitioners that the journey of the soul extends beyond the material realm, and that through a life lived in accordance with asha, they draw closer to the eternal truth of Ahura Mazda.

Asha Vahishta, or "Best Truth," is perhaps the most closely connected to the concept of asha itself. This spirit embodies the ideal of cosmic order, truth, and righteousness, serving as the very foundation of the universe's structure. Asha Vahishta is the guiding light that leads the soul toward the highest understanding of the divine plan, offering clarity and direction in the face of confusion or temptation. For Zoroastrians, Asha Vahishta is the guardian of the sacred fire, symbolizing the purest form of truth that burns away all falsehood. It is through devotion to Asha Vahishta that one learns to discern the subtle movements of asha in the world and to align their life with the flow of the divine order.

Each of these Amesha Spentas is not only a cosmic principle but a presence that can be directly engaged through prayer and meditation. Zoroastrian tradition teaches that by calling upon these spirits, practitioners invite their guidance and protection into their lives. For example, before embarking on a challenging task, one might invoke Vohu Manah for wisdom or Kshathra Vairya for strength and resilience. These invocations are often accompanied by the recitation of the Yashts, hymns dedicated to the Amesha Spentas, which are believed to contain the vibrational essence of each spirit's energy.

The Amesha Spentas are also seen as guardians of specific realms within creation, ensuring that the natural world functions in harmony with the divine plan. Vohu Manah watches over the animals, reflecting the purity and simplicity of their existence, while Armaiti cares for the earth itself, urging humanity to respect and protect the environment. Kshathra Vairya is linked to the sky and metals, representing the strength that supports life, while Haurvatat's presence is felt in the waters that sustain and cleanse. This guardianship reinforces the Zoroastrian belief that all aspects of the natural world are interconnected, and that through their stewardship, humanity honors the Amesha Spentas.

In human life, the influence of the Amesha Spentas can be felt as inner qualities—wisdom, devotion, strength, and compassion—that guide the actions of the faithful. Zoroastrians strive to cultivate these qualities within themselves, seeing their development as a reflection of the divine virtues embodied by the Amesha Spentas. This cultivation is not just a spiritual exercise but a way of bringing the light of Ahura Mazda into the world, ensuring that the principles of asha are not just ideals but lived realities.

The Amesha Spentas serve as companions on the spiritual journey, offering support and guidance through life's challenges and transitions. They remind the faithful that even in a world touched by the shadows of Angra Mainyu, the divine presence remains near, accessible to those who seek it with sincerity and an open heart. Through their influence, the teachings of Zoroaster become not only a philosophy but a lived experience, where each moment is an opportunity to draw closer to the source of light, to reflect the virtues of the divine, and to participate in the eternal work of creation.

By understanding and working with the Amesha Spentas, Zoroastrians learn to see their own lives as part of a greater cosmic story, where every thought, word, and deed contributes to the unfolding of asha in the world. This understanding transforms the journey of the soul, turning each challenge into a chance to embody the divine principles that sustain the universe, and each act of devotion into a step toward the ultimate reunion with Ahura Mazda's infinite light.

To truly harness the guidance of the Amesha Spentas, one must move beyond a conceptual understanding of their virtues and begin to work with their energies through dedicated spiritual practices. These divine beings offer a pathway for Zoroastrians to deepen their connection with the Divine Light, using prayers, rituals, and meditations that invite the presence of each Amesha Spenta into the practitioner's life.

The journey of working with the Amesha Spentas often begins with creating a space where their presence can be fully felt. For this, the practitioner should prepare an altar or a dedicated area in their home, facing a source of natural light or a sacred flame, which represents the purifying fire of asha. On this altar, symbols associated with each of the seven Amesha Spentas can be placed—such as a small bowl of water for Haurvatat, a stone or piece of metal for Kshathra Vairya, and fresh herbs or a small plant for Armaiti. These symbols act as physical reminders of the divine qualities each spirit embodies, and they create a focus for the mind during meditation and prayer.

A central practice for invoking the Amesha Spentas involves the recitation of the Yashts, hymns that honor the spirits and call upon their guidance. For example, the Ardibehesht Yasht is dedicated to Asha Vahishta, celebrating the purest form of truth and cosmic order. When reciting this hymn, the practitioner envisions the light of asha spreading through their body and mind, illuminating any shadows of confusion or falsehood. The words of the Yasht are spoken slowly, each syllable resonating with the intention to invite the presence of Asha Vahishta into their life, to guide their actions and align them with the path of righteousness.

A similar practice can be undertaken with the Bahram Yasht, which invokes the protective power of Kshathra Vairya. This hymn is recited with a focus on resilience and strength, asking for the divine aid needed to overcome personal challenges and to protect oneself from negative influences. The practitioner may visualize themselves surrounded by a shield of blue light, representing the protective essence of Kshathra Vairya. This light is imagined as impenetrable, a barrier that keeps out the forces of druj and fortifies the soul against doubt and fear. Through this practice, the practitioner cultivates a sense of inner strength that remains steady, even in times of adversity.

Meditation is another powerful method for connecting with the Amesha Spentas, allowing the practitioner to attune their mind to the subtle vibrations of each spirit. One such meditation involves focusing on Vohu Manah, the embodiment of the Good Mind. To begin, the practitioner sits quietly before the sacred flame, closing their eyes and breathing deeply. As they inhale, they imagine drawing in the clarity and wisdom of Vohu Manah, letting it fill their mind like a cool, refreshing breeze. With each exhale, they release any thoughts of confusion or anxiety, offering them to the flame to be transformed into light. This meditation is especially helpful during times of decision-making, as it helps the practitioner clear away mental distractions and focus on the choices that align with asha.

Armaiti, the spirit of devotion and harmony, is invoked through acts of gratitude and reverence for the natural world. Zoroastrians might offer a small ritual at dawn, pouring a few drops of blessed water into the earth while reciting prayers of thanks to Armaiti for the gifts of the land. This simple act is both a recognition of the sacredness of the earth and a way of inviting Armaiti's presence into the practitioner's life, fostering a deeper connection to the rhythms of nature. Through this practice, the practitioner learns to see the divine in the everyday, to honor the earth as a manifestation of Ahura Mazda's creation, and to align their actions with the gentle, nurturing qualities of Armaiti.

For those seeking to deepen their connection to Haurvatat and Ameretat—Wholeness and Immortality—rituals involving water are particularly effective. A common practice is the Ab-Zor purification, where the practitioner immerses their hands or feet in flowing water, such as a river or stream, while reciting the Haurvatat Yasht. As they do so, they visualize the water as a stream of light that cleanses both body and spirit, washing away impurities and renewing their connection to the eternal flow of life. This practice is believed to open the soul to the gifts of healing and spiritual renewal, helping the practitioner to feel the eternal presence of Ameretat, which transcends the cycles of life and death.

Working with the Amesha Spentas also involves a deeper alignment with the values they represent. For instance, to truly invite Asha Vahishta's guidance, one must strive to embody honesty in all interactions and to act with integrity, even when faced with difficult circumstances. This commitment is reinforced through daily self-reflection, where the practitioner reviews their actions and thoughts, asking themselves if they have lived in accordance with asha. This reflection can be performed as a silent meditation before sleep, with a candle burning beside them, representing the ever-watchful light of Asha Vahishta.

Similarly, invoking Spenta Mainyu's creative force requires an openness to new perspectives and a willingness to see the divine potential in every moment. It means recognizing that every challenge is an opportunity for spiritual growth and that each interaction can be a chance to spread light and kindness. By cultivating a mindset that seeks the good in others and in themselves, practitioners allow Spenta Mainyu to work through them, becoming co-creators with Ahura Mazda in the ongoing story of creation.

Each invocation of the Amesha Spentas is not merely a ritual but a step in an ongoing relationship with the divine. As practitioners become more attuned to these spirits, they begin to recognize their presence in the world around them—in the warmth of the sun, the flow of water, the wisdom of silence, and the strength of community. This awareness transforms daily life into a series of sacred encounters, where every moment holds the potential for divine connection and every action can be a reflection of the cosmic virtues.

In this way, the practice of invoking the Amesha Spentas becomes a profound journey of spiritual alignment. It allows practitioners to feel the presence of the divine not only during moments of prayer but throughout their everyday experiences. The energy of the Amesha Spentas becomes a guiding force that shapes their thoughts, influences their decisions, and inspires them to act with compassion and strength.

By engaging with these divine spirits, Zoroastrians create a bridge between the material world and the realm of spiritual truth. They learn to live in a state of asha, where each day is an opportunity to reflect the light of Ahura Mazda through their actions. The teachings of the Amesha Spentas remind them that they are never alone on their path—these divine companions walk beside them, offering guidance and strength as they navigate the complexities of life.

Through this deep connection, Zoroastrians embrace the promise of renewal and transformation, understanding that their journey is a part of a larger cosmic plan. By inviting the energies of the Amesha Spentas into their lives, they open themselves to the possibility of becoming vessels for the Divine Light, helping to bring forth the vision of a world where asha reigns supreme and the light of Ahura Mazda shines unimpeded through every aspect of creation.

Chapter 8
The Spiritual Journey

The spiritual path in Zoroastrianism is often described as a journey—a progression from the darkness of ignorance to the radiant understanding of the Divine Light. This journey is not linear; it is a cycle of deepening insights, trials, and revelations that guide the practitioner closer to Ahura Mazda. Each step taken in alignment with asha reinforces the connection to the divine, transforming daily life into a sacred quest for truth and purity.

For many Zoroastrians, the journey begins with the Navjote ceremony, an initiation that marks the formal acceptance of the faith. This rite of passage typically takes place in childhood, but it is a moment that resonates throughout a Zoroastrian's life, representing the commitment to live by the principles of asha. During the Navjote, the initiate is presented with the sudreh, a sacred white garment that symbolizes purity, and the kushti, a woven cord tied around the waist. These items are more than physical symbols; they are reminders of the vow to uphold truth, perform good deeds, and maintain spiritual vigilance against the forces of druj. The Navjote serves as a gateway, opening the path to a lifetime of spiritual practice and devotion.

The initial stage of the spiritual journey is often characterized by a focus on learning and understanding the teachings of Zoroaster. This involves studying the Gathas—the hymns of Zoroaster that contain the core teachings of the faith. Through these ancient verses, practitioners gain insight into the dualistic struggle between asha (truth) and druj (falsehood), the nature of the soul, and the role of humanity in upholding the divine order. This phase is akin to planting seeds; it is a time of absorbing knowledge, laying the foundation for a deeper spiritual awareness that will grow with time.

Yet, the path is not without its trials. As the practitioner moves beyond the initial enthusiasm of discovery, they encounter the complexities of applying these teachings in daily life. It is here that the internal struggle becomes most evident—where the desires of the material world and the whispers of Angra Mainyu challenge the clarity of asha. Doubt may arise, as well as feelings of inadequacy in living up to the ideals set forth in the Gathas. Zoroastrian teachings recognize this stage as a necessary part of the spiritual journey, a time when the individual learns to navigate their inner landscape and confront the shadows within.

The kushti ritual becomes especially important during these moments of internal conflict. By reciting the Kem Na Mazda prayer while retying the kushti, the practitioner reaffirms their connection to Ahura Mazda and their commitment to resisting the forces of druj. This simple act serves as a grounding practice, a way to regain focus and remember the vows made during the Navjote. It transforms everyday challenges into opportunities for spiritual growth, reminding the practitioner that each choice, no matter how small, is a step on the path toward the Light Divine.

As the journey deepens, the practitioner begins to focus more on the cultivation of virtues. The Zoroastrian triad of Humata (Good Thoughts), Hukhta (Good Words), and Hvarshta (Good Deeds) becomes not only a guide but a daily discipline. The practice of good thoughts involves a conscious effort to shape the mind in alignment with asha, replacing negativity with kindness, understanding, and clarity. This discipline extends into the realm of speech, where the practitioner strives to speak truthfully and with compassion, recognizing that words have the power to create or destroy, to heal or to harm.

Good deeds, or Hvarshta, are seen as the natural outflow of a mind and heart attuned to asha. This stage of the journey emphasizes action—helping those in need, supporting the community, and protecting the environment as manifestations of devotion to Ahura Mazda. These actions are not viewed as mere duties but as sacred expressions of one's role in the cosmic order. Through these deeds, the practitioner contributes to the unfolding of asha in the world, creating ripples of light that extend beyond their immediate circumstances.

As the practitioner continues to integrate these virtues, they enter a phase of greater spiritual awareness, where the presence of the divine becomes more palpable in their daily life. Meditation on the sacred fire and the practice of Atash Bandagi help deepen this awareness, allowing the practitioner to experience the inner light that mirrors the eternal flame of Ahura Mazda. This stage is characterized by a sense of inner peace and a growing ability to perceive the presence of the Amesha Spentas as guides and protectors. It is a time when the boundaries between the material and spiritual worlds begin to blur, revealing the underlying unity of all creation.

Yet even in this phase of deepened understanding, challenges remain. Zoroastrians believe that spiritual progress can attract the attention of Angra Mainyu, who seeks to disrupt the connection between the soul and the Divine Light. These challenges often manifest as subtle temptations—pride in one's progress, complacency in spiritual practice, or the temptation to judge others. To navigate these obstacles, the practitioner turns to the protective prayers like the Ahuna Vairya, which reinforces the commitment to truth and renews the strength needed to continue the journey. This period of testing is seen as a refining process, a way of purifying the soul further so that it can become a clearer vessel for the light of asha.

An important aspect of this journey is the community's role in supporting the individual's progress. The presence of elders, priests, and fellow practitioners offers guidance and encouragement, creating a sense of solidarity in the shared struggle against druj. Community prayers and rituals, such as the Yasna ceremonies conducted in the fire temples, provide moments of collective devotion, strengthening the spiritual resolve of each member. In these gatherings, the flames of the sacred fire reflect not only the light of Ahura Mazda but also the united intention of the faithful to uphold asha in a world that often feels fragmented and uncertain.

The journey continues into later stages of life, where the focus shifts towards a deepening sense of surrender to the divine will. The practitioner learns to trust in the unfolding of asha, accepting the ebb and flow of fortune with equanimity. This phase is often accompanied by a sense of gratitude, a recognition that each challenge and triumph has contributed to their spiritual growth. It is a time of turning inward, reflecting on the journey that has been traveled, and preparing the soul for its eventual transition beyond the physical world.

As the end of life approaches, Zoroastrians view this time not with fear, but with a sense of readiness, understanding that death is another stage in the journey toward Ahura Mazda. The soul, having strived to live in alignment with asha, prepares to cross the Chinvat Bridge, where its deeds will be weighed. The teachings of Zoroastrianism provide a comforting assurance that a life lived in service to truth, compassion, and justice will lead to a reunion with the Divine Light, entering the eternal realms of Frashokereti, the final renewal of the world.

The spiritual journey of a Zoroastrian is thus one of constant transformation, where every moment holds the potential for growth, renewal, and a closer communion with Ahura Mazda. It is a path that challenges and refines, that asks for both strength and humility. Through the trials of life and the joys of spiritual insight, the Zoroastrian learns to see the world not as a place of separation but as a living expression of divine order—a place where every action, thought, and breath can be an offering to the Light Divine.

For those on the Zoroastrian spiritual path, structuring a daily practice is essential to maintaining and deepening their connection with the Divine Light. The journey is not defined by isolated moments of enlightenment, but by the steady rhythm of daily devotion and reflection.

One of the most fundamental practices in the daily life of a Zoroastrian is the recitation of prayers, which serve as both a connection to the divine and a means of reinforcing the principles of asha. The day is divided into five prayer times, known as Gahs, each aligned with a different part of the day: dawn, midday, afternoon, sunset, and night. These prayers are not merely acts of devotion but opportunities to realign with the cosmic order, pausing amidst daily activities to reflect on the presence of Ahura Mazda.

Morning prayers, such as the Hoshbam and the Ahuna Vairya, set the tone for the day, inviting the light of the sun and the light of asha into the practitioner's mind and heart. As the sun rises, the practitioner recites these prayers facing the light, allowing its warmth to remind them of the divine radiance that guides their path. This morning ritual is often accompanied by a few moments of silent meditation, where the focus is on visualizing the rays of the sun as streams of pure energy that cleanse the mind of any lingering shadows, filling it with clarity and purpose.

Midday prayer is a time for renewal. In the heat of the day, when the world is most active, the practitioner takes a moment to recite the Ashem Vohu, a prayer that reinforces the importance of truth and the strength needed to uphold it. This prayer is short but potent, a reminder that even in the midst of busyness, the connection to asha remains central. The practitioner might also take this time to reflect on their actions so far, considering whether their thoughts, words, and deeds have aligned with the ideals of good thoughts, good words, and good actions.

Evening prayers, such as the Sarosh Baj or the Yasna, help to close the day with gratitude and reflection. As the sun sets, the practitioner faces the west, honoring the transition from light to darkness while reaffirming their commitment to the light within. This time of prayer is also a moment to offer thanks to the Amesha Spentas for their guidance throughout the day and to ask for protection during the night, when the forces of Angra Mainyu are believed to be more active. This evening ritual helps to anchor the practitioner in a sense of peace, knowing that their actions throughout the day have been aligned with their spiritual path.

Beyond these formal prayer times, the practice of Atash Bandagi—meditation on the sacred fire—becomes a daily refuge for those seeking to deepen their connection with the Divine Light. This practice can be done at any time when the practitioner feels the need to center themselves. Sitting before a flame or candle, they focus on the steady glow, letting their mind merge with the purity of the fire. The practitioner breathes deeply, inhaling the warmth and vitality of the flame, and exhales any thoughts that cloud their mind. This meditation is particularly useful for quieting the mind after a challenging day, allowing the practitioner to release tension and return to a state of inner balance.

The Kushti ritual, the act of untying and retying the sacred cord, is another key element of the Zoroastrian daily routine. Practiced upon waking, before meals, and before sleep, it serves as a constant reminder of the commitments made during the Navjote initiation. Each time the kushti is retied, the practitioner recites the Kem Na Mazda, a prayer that calls for Ahura Mazda's protection against the forces of druj. This simple ritual is a way of weaving the principles of asha into the fabric of everyday life, ensuring that the practitioner's intentions remain aligned with the divine throughout the day.

For those seeking to deepen their practice, additional time can be devoted to the study of the Avesta, the holy scriptures of Zoroastrianism. Reading passages from the Gathas or the Yashts allows practitioners to meditate on the teachings of Zoroaster and the words of ancient wisdom. This study can be followed by a period of silent reflection, where the practitioner considers how these teachings apply to their own life and the challenges they face. Over time, this practice of study and contemplation fosters a deeper understanding of the spiritual journey, allowing the teachings to become a living presence in the practitioner's thoughts and actions.

Creating a dedicated space for these practices is also essential. This space might include an altar with a small fire or candle, symbols of the Amesha Spentas, and sacred texts. The atmosphere of this space is kept clean and serene, free from distractions. It is a place where the practitioner can retreat from the noise of the world and reconnect with the inner light. Over time, this space becomes a sanctuary that holds the accumulated energy of devotion, a place where the presence of Ahura Mazda feels especially close.

The rhythm of daily practice is not meant to be rigid; it can be adapted to the flow of life, accommodating the varying demands of work, family, and community. Zoroastrian teachings emphasize the importance of intention over formality. If a day's responsibilities make it difficult to follow every prayer or meditation precisely, the practitioner focuses instead on maintaining an inner attitude of reverence and gratitude. A simple heartfelt prayer whispered in the midst of daily tasks can carry as much spiritual power as a formal recitation if it is offered with sincerity.

As the practitioner advances along the spiritual path, the focus of these daily practices begins to shift from self-discipline to a deeper experience of surrender and trust in the divine. In these moments, prayer becomes less about asking for guidance and more about listening for the quiet voice of Ahura Mazda within. The practitioner learns to recognize signs of divine presence in everyday life—a kind word, a beautiful sunset, the steady flame of a candle—and to see these moments as invitations to deepen their connection to the sacred.

These practices also help the practitioner to face challenges with a spirit of resilience and faith. When difficulties arise—whether they are external events or internal struggles—Zoroastrians are encouraged to see these moments as opportunities to strengthen their resolve. Reciting the Ahuna Vairya during times of fear or doubt, meditating on the light of the fire when facing uncertainty, or performing acts of kindness even when burdened by grief—all of these actions transform hardship into a process of spiritual refinement.

The daily spiritual routine of a Zoroastrian is a testament to the belief that the divine is always present, that the path to Ahura Mazda is found not only in grand rituals but in the small, steady acts of devotion that shape everyday life. Through these practices, the practitioner learns to carry the light of asha within them, letting it illuminate their thoughts, words, and deeds. This inner light becomes a guide, helping them navigate the complexities of the world while staying true to the path of truth and compassion.

Ultimately, the goal of these practices is to create a life that is in constant dialogue with the divine—a life where each breath, each moment, is an opportunity to affirm one's commitment to asha and to participate in the unfolding of the cosmic order. By embracing this rhythm of daily devotion, the Zoroastrian practitioner turns their life into a vessel for the Light Divine, embodying the ancient teachings of Zoroaster in a way that is both timeless and deeply personal.

Chapter 9
The Practice of Charity

In Zoroastrianism, the practice of charity (Dāna) holds a special place, embodying the principles of asha through acts of kindness, generosity, and compassion. Charity is not merely seen as a moral obligation but as a profound spiritual practice that connects the practitioner to the divine essence of Ahura Mazda. Through charity, Zoroastrians manifest the virtues of Spenta Mainyu, the Beneficent Spirit, which opposes the chaos and division sown by Angra Mainyu. It is through such acts that one becomes a living channel of the Divine Light, spreading it throughout the world and fostering a sense of unity and balance.

The concept of charity in Zoroastrianism extends beyond material gifts; it encompasses a broader understanding of service and the sharing of spiritual and emotional support. Zoroaster's teachings emphasize that good thoughts, good words, and good deeds (Humata, Hukhta, Hvarshta) are the foundation of a righteous life. Thus, charity is not confined to the giving of physical goods but includes offering one's time, wisdom, and energy to uplift others. It is about recognizing the needs of those around us and responding with an open heart, whether through providing shelter, offering a listening ear, or simply sharing a kind word that brightens someone's day.

In Zoroastrian tradition, the act of giving is deeply connected to the concept of Spenta Armaiti, or Holy Devotion. Armaiti encourages an attitude of selflessness and humility, guiding practitioners to view all beings as part of the divine creation deserving of care and respect. This spiritual perspective transforms charity into a sacred duty, a way of honoring the divine presence within others. It teaches that through service to others, one serves Ahura Mazda, reinforcing the bonds of community and creating a world that is more aligned with the principles of asha.

The teachings of the Gathas, Zoroaster's sacred hymns, stress that acts of charity contribute to the cosmic struggle between asha (order) and druj (deceit). When a Zoroastrian engages in charity, they actively push back against the forces of druj, which seek to create division, poverty, and suffering. By alleviating the burdens of others, the practitioner reduces the influence of negativity in the world, replacing it with compassion and support. This understanding adds a cosmic significance to every charitable act, turning even the simplest gesture of kindness into a contribution to the divine plan.

One of the most important aspects of charity in Zoroastrianism is the practice of hospitality, or mehmaan-dari. Traditionally, Zoroastrians are taught to treat every guest as a manifestation of divine presence. The home is seen as a place where the light of asha should shine brightly, and welcoming others with warmth and generosity is a way of expressing that light. Offering food, shelter, and comfort to guests is considered an act of worship in itself, reflecting the values of Spenta Mainyu, who embodies the qualities of nurturing and care. The offering of hospitality becomes a way to strengthen community bonds, creating spaces where the light of asha can flourish.

Charity also plays a significant role in Zoroastrian festivals and holy days, such as Nowruz, the Persian New Year. During this time, families prepare meals not only for themselves but also for those in need, ensuring that no one is left without the means to celebrate the renewal of life. This spirit of giving during Nowruz symbolizes the victory of light over darkness, mirroring the renewal of the earth in spring and the promise of asha's ultimate triumph over druj. The act of sharing during these communal celebrations reinforces the idea that abundance is meant to be shared, creating a cycle of generosity that extends beyond the self.

For Zoroastrians, the intention behind charitable actions is as important as the actions themselves. True charity, as taught by Zoroaster, comes from a place of sincerity and a desire to connect with the divine within others. It is not motivated by the hope of reward or recognition but by the understanding that every soul is interconnected. When giving is done with a pure heart, it is said to strengthen the soul's khvarenah—its inner light and spiritual glory—bringing the practitioner closer to the essence of Ahura Mazda. This belief encourages practitioners to approach charity as an opportunity for spiritual growth, as much as it is an opportunity to serve.

A key ritual associated with charity is the Barashnum, a purification rite that can accompany acts of giving. The Barashnum is traditionally performed with the recitation of the Ashem Vohu prayer, which emphasizes the importance of truth and righteousness. Before giving, the practitioner washes their hands in flowing water, symbolizing the cleansing of any impurities of intention, and offers a silent prayer that their gift may bring true benefit to the recipient. This ritual transforms the act of giving into a moment of connection with asha, ensuring that the energy of the gift is aligned with the highest good.

In addition to material charity, Zoroastrian teachings emphasize the importance of sharing knowledge and wisdom. This aspect of charity, known as Kherad-gahi, involves offering guidance, mentorship, and support to those who seek it, especially the young and the uninitiated in the teachings of Zoroaster. Sharing spiritual teachings, providing moral guidance, or simply offering words of encouragement is considered a way to spread the light of asha through the community. It ensures that the wisdom of the ancient texts remains alive, passing from generation to generation, and that each person has the opportunity to walk the path of light.

Charity is also seen as a form of resistance against the influence of Angra Mainyu, who seeks to create division and suffering among people. By practicing charity, Zoroastrians actively build a world that reflects the principles of unity and harmony. This is evident in the concept of Hamazor, which emphasizes the power of standing together in strength and fellowship. Hamazor is not just a greeting or a word—it is a spiritual bond that signifies mutual support and solidarity. When communities gather resources to help those in need, they are practicing Hamazor, standing together against the forces of darkness and creating a space where the Divine Light can flourish.

The practice of charity in Zoroastrianism thus extends far beyond mere almsgiving; it is an integral part of the faith's vision of a world aligned with the divine order. It transforms the ordinary act of giving into a sacred ritual, a means of expressing the divine qualities of compassion and nurturing. Through charity, Zoroastrians engage directly in the work of asha, fostering a world where the well-being of each individual contributes to the well-being of all.

By embracing this practice, the Zoroastrian learns to see their resources—whether material, spiritual, or emotional—not as possessions to be guarded, but as blessings to be shared. Each act of generosity, no matter how small, is a reminder that the light of Ahura Mazda flows through all beings, connecting each to the other. In this way, charity becomes a daily practice that shapes the practitioner's view of the world, turning every encounter into an opportunity to bring a little more light, a little more asha, into the lives of those they touch.

Through the lens of charity, Zoroastrianism teaches that the true wealth of a person is not measured by what they hold, but by what they give. This perspective transforms the material world into a field of spiritual opportunity, where the flow of resources mirrors the flow of divine energy. By giving freely, the Zoroastrian not only helps others but also participates in the larger work of maintaining the cosmic balance, ensuring that the path of asha continues to shine brightly for all.

In deepening the practice of charity, Zoroastrian teachings encourage not only spontaneous acts of kindness but also a structured approach to giving that is woven into the fabric of daily life.

One foundational practice is the concept of Mithra, or the spirit of truth and promise. In Zoroastrianism, making a vow to support others, whether through regular charitable donations or offering time to community service, carries a deep spiritual weight. When a Zoroastrian makes such a vow, it is seen as a contract not only with the recipient but with the divine, reflecting the commitment to uphold asha. Keeping these promises, no matter how small, strengthens the practitioner's integrity and their connection to the divine, turning each act of charity into an expression of spiritual discipline.

A practical way to incorporate charity into daily life is through the creation of a Dāna jar—a small container where the practitioner places a portion of their income or resources as a dedicated fund for helping those in need. Each time they add to the jar, they recite the Ashem Vohu or Yatha Ahu Vairyo prayers, offering gratitude for the opportunity to give and asking for the blessings of Ahura Mazda upon those who will receive their aid. This simple practice turns the act of giving into a ritual, reminding the practitioner that their resources are a means to serve the light. When the jar is full, the funds can be used to support a local charity, assist a struggling neighbor, or contribute to community projects.

Another significant practice is the Mahr-e-Mithra, which involves setting aside a portion of one's meals or harvest to be shared with the less fortunate. In traditional Zoroastrian communities, families often prepare extra food during meals, knowing that some of it will be offered to those who might come to their door. This practice is especially emphasized during holy days and festivals, such as Nowruz, where the abundance of the season is shared as a symbol of renewal and hope. Preparing food with the intention of sharing not only fulfills a social need but also transforms the meal itself into a sacred offering, a gesture that embodies the spirit of Armaiti, the Amesha Spenta of devotion and love.

For those seeking to engage more directly with their community, Hamazor circles—groups of individuals coming together to pool resources for charitable projects—provide a structured way to practice collective generosity. These circles often focus on specific needs within the community, such as providing education for children, assisting families in times of crisis, or organizing clean-up drives in local parks and rivers, reflecting the Zoroastrian reverence for nature. The act of giving through these circles is seen as a way of strengthening the bonds of fellowship, where each member contributes according to their ability, creating a shared pool of resources that reflects the unity of purpose in the fight against druj.

Zoroastrian teachings also emphasize the importance of anonymous charity—giving without seeking recognition or praise. This approach to charity is rooted in the belief that the true value of a gift lies in its intention, not in the acknowledgment it receives. Anonymous giving allows the practitioner to focus purely on the act of service, offering their aid as a silent prayer to Ahura Mazda for the well-being of others. This practice reflects the Zoroastrian ideal of humility, recognizing that the act of giving is itself a gift from the divine, an opportunity to participate in the cosmic flow of abundance and kindness.

To aid in cultivating a mindset of continual generosity, Zoroastrians are encouraged to begin each day with a Dāna meditation, focusing on gratitude for the blessings they have received and the desire to share those blessings with others. This meditation involves sitting quietly, visualizing the light of Ahura Mazda filling their heart, and imagining that light expanding outward, touching those who are in need. As the light spreads, the practitioner reflects on specific actions they can take that day to bring relief or joy to others, whether through a kind word, a small donation, or an act of service. This practice helps to align the mind with the principles of asha, turning the intention of charity into a guiding force throughout the day.

In addition to these practices, Zoroastrian teachings provide specific prayers that can be offered for the well-being of those who are suffering or in need. The Fravardin Yasht, dedicated to the Fravashis (guardian spirits), is often recited as a way of asking for protection and support for those who face hardship. During the recitation, the practitioner lights a candle or incense, allowing the smoke to rise as a symbol of their prayers reaching the divine realm. As they pray, they focus on the faces of those they wish to help, sending their thoughts of compassion and healing through the spiritual connection they hold with the Fravashis. This prayer is believed to create a network of support between the visible and invisible worlds, offering strength and comfort to those in need.

Zoroastrians are also taught that the spirit of charity extends beyond human interactions to encompass all living beings. Acts of kindness towards animals and care for the environment are seen as expressions of asha. This belief is rooted in the idea that every part of creation carries the essence of the Divine Light. Offering food to birds during winter, ensuring clean water sources for animals, or planting trees in areas affected by deforestation are all seen as acts of service to Ahura Mazda's creation. Through these actions, the practitioner not only fulfills their duty to the earth but also experiences a deeper connection to the natural world, recognizing the divine presence that flows through all life.

The practice of charity in Zoroastrianism thus creates a sacred rhythm within daily life, where the act of giving becomes a constant conversation with the divine. It turns every opportunity to help into a moment of spiritual reflection, a chance to remember that through generosity, the soul is polished, its light shining brighter each time it aligns with the principles of compassion and truth. This understanding transforms the world around the practitioner into a place where every encounter is a potential exchange of light, where the mundane becomes a vessel for the sacred.

As practitioners cultivate this mindset, they find that the boundaries between giver and receiver begin to dissolve. In the act of charity, both are blessed, as the one who gives learns the joy of selflessness, and the one who receives is reminded of the presence of asha even in times of need. This dynamic creates a continuous flow of spiritual energy, where the blessings of Ahura Mazda are not hoarded but passed on, keeping the light circulating within the community.

Through these structured practices, Zoroastrians come to see charity not as a burden or a duty, but as a natural expression of their connection to the divine. It becomes a way to participate in the divine dance of creation, where each act of giving mirrors the endless generosity of Ahura Mazda, who sustains the cosmos with love and wisdom. The practice of charity allows them to live in a state of grace, turning their hands into instruments of the divine, their words into vessels of kindness, and their hearts into beacons of light.

In this way, charity becomes a bridge that connects the individual soul to the larger cosmic order. It ensures that each person, regardless of their circumstances, has a role to play in the struggle between light and darkness. By embracing the principles of generosity, Zoroastrians weave themselves into the tapestry of asha, ensuring that the light of Ahura Mazda flows not only within their own hearts but also into the lives of those they touch. Through charity, the Zoroastrian path becomes one of active participation in the unfolding of the divine vision, where the world is gradually transformed into a place where love, compassion, and truth can shine ever more brightly.

Chapter 10
Worship of Nature

The Zoroastrian relationship with nature is one of reverence and deep spiritual significance, seeing the natural world as a manifestation of Ahura Mazda's divine creation. For Zoroastrians, nature is not merely a backdrop to human life, but a living tapestry woven with the energies of the Divine Light. Every element—earth, water, fire, air—carries a spark of the divine, reflecting the harmony and balance that asha seeks to maintain in the cosmos.

Central to Zoroastrian beliefs is the idea that each element of nature is a gift from Ahura Mazda, deserving of protection and care. The earth (Zam), water (Ap), fire (Atar), and plants (Urvar) are not only physical substances but spiritual entities that participate in the cosmic order. Zoroastrians believe that humans have a duty to maintain the purity of these elements, as they are essential to the balance of asha. This responsibility is reflected in ancient Zoroastrian scriptures, such as the Avesta, which contains hymns praising the earth and water and offering thanks for their life-giving properties.

Fire, perhaps the most revered of all natural elements in Zoroastrianism, is seen as a direct manifestation of the Divine Light. The sacred fire, or Atash, represents purity, truth, and the spiritual presence of Ahura Mazda. In Zoroastrian temples, fire is tended with great care, symbolizing the eternal flame of asha that burns within the cosmos. This reverence for fire extends beyond the temple; even in the home, the fire that cooks meals or provides warmth is treated with respect, seen as a symbol of the divine energy that sustains life. By maintaining the purity of fire and avoiding pollution, Zoroastrians honor their connection to Ahura Mazda and the greater cosmic order.

Water (Ap), too, holds a place of profound importance. It is considered the source of life, a symbol of purity and spiritual renewal. Zoroastrian rituals often include the use of water for purification, such as the Ab-Zor ceremony, where water is blessed and used to cleanse the body and spirit. Practitioners are taught to treat rivers, lakes, and wells with respect, avoiding actions that might pollute or harm these sacred sources. The Avan Yasht, a hymn dedicated to the waters, celebrates their power to purify and nourish, invoking the protection and blessing of Ap for the community. This respect for water aligns with the belief that maintaining the purity of natural elements is a way of upholding asha in the physical world.

Earth (Zam) is revered as the nurturing foundation upon which all life rests. Zoroastrians see the earth as a mother figure, offering her bounty and stability to those who respect her. This understanding leads to a practice of careful cultivation and stewardship of the land, ensuring that its resources are used wisely and not depleted. Traditional Zoroastrian communities practice sustainable agriculture, planting crops in accordance with the cycles of the seasons and giving thanks for each harvest. Even in urban settings, Zoroastrians strive to maintain gardens or green spaces, honoring the earth by creating small sanctuaries where life can flourish. This connection to the earth is also expressed through rituals such as the Jashan ceremony, where offerings are made to thank Zam for her abundance and support.

Plants (Urvar), representing the growth and renewal inherent in the natural world, are considered sacred as well. Zoroastrian traditions include the planting of trees and the care for plant life as acts of spiritual significance. The planting of a tree, for example, is seen as a direct contribution to the cosmic balance, offering a home to wildlife and helping to purify the air. Zoroastrians are encouraged to cultivate gardens not only for their beauty or utility but as living expressions of the divine energy that flows through all creation. Rituals involving plants, such as the use of fragrant herbs like Haoma in prayer ceremonies, acknowledge their role as intermediaries between the human and divine realms, helping to bridge the gap between the physical and spiritual worlds.

Living in harmony with these elements is not just about maintaining their physical purity; it is about understanding the spiritual lessons they offer. Each element teaches a different aspect of asha. Fire instructs on the importance of clarity and spiritual vigilance, as its flames consume impurities. Water teaches adaptability and the need for spiritual cleansing, flowing and renewing life wherever it touches. The earth offers lessons in patience and nurturing, as it sustains life through cycles of growth and decay. Plants embody resilience and the continual renewal of life, even in the face of adversity. By aligning with these natural rhythms, Zoroastrians learn to see their lives as part of the greater cosmic dance, guided by the principles of order and harmony.

The relationship with nature in Zoroastrianism also involves a recognition of the sacred spaces where the elements converge. Mountains, rivers, and forests are seen as places where the divine presence is especially close, where the veil between the physical and spiritual worlds is thin. These locations are often chosen for meditation, prayer, and rituals, allowing practitioners to immerse themselves in the energy of creation. In such settings, Zoroastrians recite the Avesta or meditate on the sacred hymns, seeking to deepen their connection with the Divine Light through the beauty and tranquility of the natural world. These practices serve as reminders that the world itself is a temple, and that every step taken on the earth is an opportunity to honor the divine.

Respecting the natural world is also seen as a form of resistance against the forces of druj, which thrive in pollution, destruction, and disorder. Zoroastrians believe that by protecting nature, they are actively fighting against the influence of Angra Mainyu, the spirit of chaos and corruption. Acts like cleaning a polluted river, planting trees in a barren area, or educating others about the importance of environmental stewardship are all viewed as sacred duties. Through these actions, Zoroastrians help to restore the balance of asha, contributing to the overall health and harmony of the world. In this way, environmental care becomes not just a social responsibility but a deeply spiritual act, a way of participating in the cosmic struggle between light and darkness.

The emphasis on the sacredness of nature is not only about honoring what is, but also about preserving the world for future generations. Zoroastrian teachings stress that the earth is a gift to be guarded, ensuring that its beauty and resources are available for those who come after us. This sense of intergenerational responsibility encourages Zoroastrians to think long-term in their interactions with the environment, considering how their actions today will impact the world tomorrow. This perspective cultivates a sense of humility and stewardship, recognizing that human beings are not the owners of the earth, but its caretakers, entrusted with its well-being by Ahura Mazda.

Ultimately, the Zoroastrian reverence for nature serves as a reminder of the interconnectedness of all life. It teaches that every element, no matter how small, holds a place in the divine plan and that by living in harmony with nature, humans can align themselves more fully with the path of asha. This alignment opens the way for a deeper connection with Ahura Mazda, allowing the practitioner to experience the Divine Light not only in moments of prayer but in the everyday miracles of wind, water, sunlight, and soil. Through this relationship with nature, Zoroastrians find a source of inspiration and strength, a living testament to the presence of the divine in all things, and a constant call to walk the path of truth, compassion, and care.

To deepen the practice of nature worship within Zoroastrianism, practitioners are encouraged to integrate specific rituals and meditative practices that foster a direct connection with the elements. These rituals are not just acts of devotion but pathways to experience the divine energy that permeates the natural world. By consciously engaging with earth, water, fire, and air, practitioners can transform their surroundings into a space of spiritual resonance, where the Divine Light of Ahura Mazda can be felt in every breath, every breeze, and every flowing stream.

One of the simplest yet profound ways to engage with nature is through the Ab-Zor ritual, a practice of water purification that can be performed at rivers, lakes, or even at home with a bowl of pure water. To begin, the practitioner finds a peaceful spot by the water, a place where they can feel the rhythm of the flow. Kneeling beside the water, they offer a prayer from the Avan Yasht, dedicating their thoughts to the sacred nature of water and asking for its blessings. With hands cupped, they lift the water, allowing it to trickle back into the source, symbolizing the renewal of the self through the purity of the water. This act becomes a moment of reflection, where the practitioner meditates on the qualities of water—its adaptability, its ability to cleanse and nourish. As they feel the coolness of the water, they envision their spirit being cleansed of impurities, aligning more closely with the path of asha.

For those who live near rivers or the sea, an offering of flowers or herbs can be added to the water as a gesture of gratitude. It is customary to choose natural materials that will not harm the water's ecosystem, such as petals from a garden or dried herbs. As these offerings are placed into the water, the practitioner recites the Ashem Vohu, acknowledging the truth and purity that flow through all of creation. This ritual, simple yet deeply symbolic, allows the practitioner to feel a direct connection to the living spirit of water and to carry that sense of renewal back into their daily life.

Another important practice is the Atash Niyayesh, a prayer of reverence for fire that can be performed outdoors in the presence of a small flame or even a campfire. For this ritual, the practitioner creates a small fire in a safe, prepared space, ideally using wood or other natural materials. As the flames rise, they recite verses from the Atash Nyash, the hymn to fire, focusing their mind on the qualities of fire as a manifestation of the Divine Light. The warmth and glow of the flames are seen as a direct link to Ahura Mazda, providing not only physical warmth but also spiritual illumination.

During this ritual, the practitioner might offer small pieces of sandalwood or other fragrant woods into the fire, symbolizing the dedication of their own impurities to be consumed and transformed. As the wood burns, the practitioner visualizes their worries and negative thoughts dissolving in the smoke, leaving behind a clearer, purer state of mind. This practice can be especially powerful at dawn or dusk, times of transition that mirror the eternal struggle between light and darkness in the cosmos. The Atash Niyayesh serves as a reminder that the flame of asha is always present, even in the darkest moments, and that by tending this inner fire, the practitioner can remain aligned with the divine.

For those who seek to deepen their connection with the earth, the Zam Jashan ritual offers a way to honor the ground beneath their feet. This ritual is often performed in gardens, fields, or any open space where the earth is visible and accessible. To begin, the practitioner clears a small area of earth, creating a space that is clean and free of debris. Kneeling on this spot, they place a few grains or seeds into the earth, offering them as a symbol of gratitude for the sustenance the earth provides. As they plant the seeds, they recite prayers from the Khorshed Yasht, asking for the blessings of the sun to nourish the earth and bring forth new life.

The act of planting seeds is both a literal and symbolic gesture, representing the hope for growth and the renewal of the earth's abundance. As the seeds are covered with soil, the practitioner meditates on the cycles of nature—growth, decay, and rebirth—and reflects on how these cycles mirror their own spiritual journey. This ritual teaches patience and trust in the process of life, as the practitioner tends to the seeds in the days and weeks that follow, watching as new life emerges from the soil. It is a way of grounding oneself in the rhythms of nature, finding peace in the slow and steady unfolding of asha through the earth's gifts.

In addition to these specific rituals, Zoroastrianism encourages meditative practices that can be performed in natural settings to deepen the sense of unity with the elements. One such practice is Wind Meditation, a form of contemplation that focuses on the breath and the movement of the air. To practice this, the individual finds a quiet place, ideally outdoors where they can feel the breeze. They sit comfortably, closing their eyes, and begin to synchronize their breath with the rhythm of the wind. Inhaling deeply, they imagine drawing in the purity of the air, and with each exhale, they release tension and thoughts that cloud the mind.

As they continue this meditation, the practitioner allows their awareness to expand, feeling themselves as part of the air that moves around them. The boundaries between their body and the surrounding space begin to dissolve, and they sense the breath as a bridge between the inner world and the vastness of the sky. This practice helps to cultivate a sense of lightness and openness, inviting the practitioner to experience the freedom and clarity that the element of air represents. It is a moment to remember that, like the wind, the spirit is free to move, adapt, and find new perspectives.

Another profound way to honor nature is through the practice of silent walks, where the practitioner moves slowly through a natural setting, focusing on the sights, sounds, and sensations around them. During these walks, no words are spoken; instead, the practitioner listens to the voice of nature—the rustling of leaves, the call of birds, the whispering of water. This practice, known as Hushidaran, teaches reverence for the living world and invites the practitioner to see the divine presence in every leaf and stone. It becomes a form of moving meditation, where each step is taken mindfully, and each breath is a prayer of connection to the earth.

Hushidaran helps to cultivate a deep sense of gratitude and presence, allowing the practitioner to experience nature not as a distant reality but as a sacred space that is alive with the energy of Ahura Mazda. These walks can be done at any time, but they are particularly powerful at sunrise or sunset, when the changing light creates a sense of transformation and renewal. Through this practice, the practitioner learns to see themselves as a part of nature's cycle, embracing both their smallness and their integral place within the web of life.

Chapter 11
Cosmic Consciousness

In Zoroastrianism, the concept of Cosmic Consciousness serves as a gateway to a deeper understanding of the interconnectedness that binds all existence. It is a profound spiritual awareness that allows practitioners to perceive the universe not merely as a collection of isolated entities, but as a living, breathing whole—one that pulses with the essence of Ahura Mazda's divine light. This consciousness is both a goal and a practice, guiding the Zoroastrian on a journey beyond the limits of the individual self, toward a profound unity with the cosmos.

The seeds of this idea are found in the teachings of Zoroaster, who spoke of asha—the cosmic order that governs the universe. Asha is not only a moral code but a principle that underlies the entire fabric of existence, maintaining harmony between all beings and the natural world. To attune oneself to asha is to recognize the underlying thread that connects the movements of stars, the cycles of nature, and the inner workings of the human soul. Through this recognition, one begins to see the universe as an intricate dance of light and energy, with each element playing a role in a greater divine symphony.

Achieving a state of Cosmic Consciousness requires a shift in perspective, moving from the individual-centered view to one that encompasses a broader, universal vision. It begins with the understanding that the soul (urvan) is not confined to the body but is an expression of a greater, eternal reality. The Fravashi—often translated as "guardian spirit"—is believed to be the higher aspect of the soul, one that remains connected to the divine source even as the urvan navigates the physical world. By aligning with the wisdom of the Fravashi, the practitioner can tap into a deeper stream of awareness, one that flows from Ahura Mazda's own vision for the universe.

Meditation is a key practice for cultivating Cosmic Consciousness, helping to quiet the mind and open it to the subtler currents of reality. One effective technique is the Hushmori meditation, where the practitioner focuses on the silent intervals between breaths. As the breath flows in and out, the practitioner pays special attention to the moments of stillness between the inhalation and exhalation, allowing their awareness to expand into this space of quiet. In this state of silence, the barriers between the self and the universe begin to dissolve, and the practitioner can sense the presence of asha as a gentle current that moves through all things.

Visualization is another powerful tool for expanding consciousness. In Cosmic Light Meditation, the practitioner envisions themselves standing beneath a vast night sky, where each star represents a point of divine energy. As they breathe deeply, they imagine the light of these stars flowing down into their body, filling every cell with radiant energy. With each breath, the light expands, creating a sense of unity between the body, the earth beneath, and the cosmos above. This practice helps to cultivate a feeling of being both infinitesimally small and expansively vast, a part of the universe's infinite tapestry.

This sense of interconnectedness is further deepened by the Zoroastrian practice of Hamkar, or "working together with the cosmos." Hamkar teaches that human beings are co-creators in the unfolding of asha, with every thought, word, and action contributing to the balance of the universe. It is a recognition that just as the sun rises each day, the rivers flow, and the earth renews itself, so too does each person have a role to play in the maintenance of cosmic order. By consciously choosing actions that align with asha, the practitioner becomes a participant in the great cosmic struggle against druj (chaos and deceit), ensuring that the light of truth continues to shine.

Zoroastrian teachings also speak of the Chinvat Bridge, which the soul must cross after death—a passage that symbolizes the transition from the material to the cosmic perspective. This journey over the Chinvat Bridge is not only a physical passage but a spiritual one, requiring the soul to shed the limitations of earthly concerns and embrace its place within the vastness of divine reality. It is said that those who live their lives in accordance with asha will find the bridge easy to cross, as they have already begun to perceive the unity between their actions and the cosmic order. In this way, the path toward Cosmic Consciousness begins in life and extends beyond it, guiding the soul back to its divine source.

The Gathas, the hymns of Zoroaster, offer profound insights into this journey toward universal awareness. In these sacred verses, Zoroaster often reflects on the nature of existence, the role of humanity within the cosmic plan, and the eternal struggle between light and darkness. By studying these hymns and meditating on their meanings, practitioners can gain a deeper understanding of their own place within the universe. The Gathas serve as a reminder that every moment is an opportunity to align with the greater flow of asha, transforming ordinary life into a sacred dance with the divine.

Developing Cosmic Consciousness also means cultivating a sense of empathy and connection with all living beings. The realization that all souls share the same divine spark leads to a deepened sense of compassion, not just for fellow humans but for animals, plants, and the earth itself. Zoroastrians are encouraged to see their relationships with others as reflections of their relationship with Ahura Mazda. Acts of kindness, care for the environment, and efforts to bring peace and understanding become ways of honoring the divine light that flows through all creation. This expanded awareness turns every interaction into a moment of spiritual practice, where the lines between self and other blur in the presence of the divine.

Zoroastrian cosmology teaches that time itself is part of the unfolding of asha, with the universe moving through cycles of creation, maintenance, and eventual renewal. By understanding these cycles, the practitioner gains a sense of the impermanence of material things and the eternal nature of the spiritual. The awareness of Zrvan Akarana—Infinite Time—helps to shift the focus from the fleeting nature of daily struggles to the enduring presence of the divine plan. It allows the practitioner to view life's challenges not as isolated events but as part of a larger, purposeful movement toward harmony and balance.

One way to connect with this cosmic perspective is through Zarvan meditation, where the practitioner contemplates the flow of time while focusing on the eternal nature of the soul. Sitting in a quiet space, they imagine time as a river, flowing through their mind and body, carrying away thoughts of the past and worries of the future. As they meditate on this flow, they become aware of the timeless presence within themselves—the part of their being that is connected to Zrvan Akarana and remains constant amidst the changes of the physical world. This meditation helps to cultivate a sense of inner stillness and acceptance, allowing the practitioner to engage with the world without losing sight of the deeper currents of existence.

The journey toward Cosmic Consciousness is not one of abandoning the self, but of expanding it to include the universe. It is a recognition that the soul is a microcosm of the larger cosmic order, and that by attuning to the divine rhythms of nature and the universe, one can find a deeper sense of purpose and peace. This consciousness opens the way to a life that is fully engaged with the present moment while remaining anchored in the eternal. It transforms the Zoroastrian's experience of reality, turning each day into a new opportunity to align with the unfolding of asha, to participate in the cosmic dance of creation, and to embrace their role as a bearer of the Divine Light.

To cultivate Cosmic Consciousness fully, Zoroastrian practitioners are encouraged to engage in deeper, more refined techniques that elevate their spiritual awareness beyond the ordinary. These advanced practices focus on expanding the mind's capacity to perceive the universe's interconnected nature, allowing the practitioner to feel the pulse of asha in every part of their being and the world around them.

One of the foundational practices for deepening Cosmic Consciousness is the Yasna Yasht meditation, a profound form of meditation where the practitioner seeks to connect directly with the energy of the stars, the celestial bodies that ancient Zoroastrians viewed as the keepers of divine order. To perform this meditation, the practitioner sits under an open sky, ideally at night, when the stars are visible. They begin by closing their eyes and taking deep, rhythmic breaths, imagining that with each inhale, they draw in the light of the stars, and with each exhale, they release any thoughts or feelings that obscure their perception.

After several minutes, the practitioner opens their eyes and focuses on a single star, allowing its distant light to become a point of concentration. As they maintain their focus, they visualize a stream of light connecting them to that star, a thread that links their soul to the vast cosmic network. Through this visualization, the practitioner contemplates the idea that every star, every point of light in the sky, is part of the same divine essence that flows through all life. They imagine themselves as a single star within this vast constellation, a point of consciousness that contributes to the greater pattern of asha. This practice helps to dissolve feelings of isolation, replacing them with a sense of belonging to the universe's endless expanse.

Another important technique for accessing Cosmic Consciousness is the Atar Zarathushtra ritual, which involves using fire as a focal point for meditation. In this practice, the practitioner lights a small, sacred fire and sits before it, allowing the warmth and glow to fill their awareness. They recite the Yatha Ahu Vairyo and Ashem Vohu prayers, dedicating their thoughts to the principles of truth and divine order. As they focus on the flames, they visualize the fire as a living connection between the physical world and the spiritual realms, a manifestation of Ahura Mazda's energy that burns away illusions and reveals the true nature of reality.

The practitioner then closes their eyes and imagines the fire expanding beyond its physical form, growing until it becomes a great cosmic flame that encompasses the entire universe. In this vision, they see galaxies, stars, and planets spinning within the fire, each one moving according to the rhythms of asha. They imagine their own soul as a part of this cosmic fire, a spark that contributes to the light and warmth of the divine creation. This practice is particularly effective for those seeking to overcome feelings of spiritual stagnation or disconnection, as it reignites the inner flame of purpose and reminds the practitioner of their place within the cosmic order.

For those who wish to deepen their understanding of time and its role in Cosmic Consciousness, the Zrvan Yasht meditation offers a way to perceive the flow of time from a spiritual perspective. In this meditation, the practitioner sits quietly, contemplating the passage of time as a river that flows both through and beyond them. They imagine the river as a golden stream that carries moments of past, present, and future, all interwoven yet distinct. As they meditate on this flow, they become aware of a timeless presence within themselves—the part of their spirit that exists beyond the confines of linear time, connected to the eternal nature of Zrvan Akarana.

The Zrvan Yasht meditation teaches that while time shapes the material world, the spirit is not bound by these constraints. By entering a state of awareness where time seems to slow or even stop, the practitioner can experience moments of clarity where they feel deeply attuned to the patterns of the universe. These moments are akin to glimpses of asha, where the complexities of life align, and the underlying harmony of existence becomes evident. This practice helps to cultivate patience and perspective, allowing the practitioner to navigate life's challenges with a sense of trust in the divine plan.

In addition to meditation and visualization, Zoroastrianism offers rituals that can be performed in natural settings to enhance Cosmic Consciousness. One such practice is the Ardvisur Yasht, a ritual performed near bodies of water, where the practitioner invokes the presence of Ardvi Sura Anahita, the spirit of the waters. This ritual begins with a simple offering—a handful of grains or flowers—to the water, along with prayers of gratitude for the life-giving properties of Ap. As the offering is made, the practitioner sits by the water, listening to its flow and allowing their thoughts to merge with the rhythm of the current.

In this state of meditation, they envision the water as a mirror that reflects the entire cosmos, with each ripple representing a different aspect of creation. They contemplate how the flow of water is like the flow of cosmic energy, moving through stars, planets, and souls. This reflection becomes a form of dialogue with the universe, where the practitioner asks for insight into their place within the cosmic order and listens for the subtle answers that arise within their heart. This ritual teaches that just as the water connects all points along its path, so too does asha connect every soul, every element of existence, into a single, harmonious whole.

To strengthen the connection between the individual and the universe, Zoroastrian teachings emphasize the importance of Sraosha, the divine messenger who bridges the gap between the spiritual and material realms. By invoking Sraosha during meditation or prayer, the practitioner can open themselves to the wisdom that flows from the higher planes. The Sraosha Yasht is a chant that calls upon this divine guide, asking for clarity and guidance in understanding the mysteries of the cosmos. As they chant, the practitioner focuses on the idea that every sound they create is a vibration that travels through space, resonating with the energy of the stars and the silent songs of creation.

The Sraosha Yasht chant serves as a reminder that human consciousness is not isolated; it is part of a vast network of spiritual currents that move through the universe. By attuning themselves to these currents, practitioners can gain insights that transcend ordinary perception, experiencing flashes of understanding that illuminate their path. This practice helps to refine the intuition, allowing the practitioner to sense the subtle movements of asha in their life and to act in harmony with the deeper rhythms of existence.

The practice of Cosmic Communion—a form of silent prayer performed at dawn or twilight—invites the practitioner to merge their awareness with the transition between night and day. Standing outside, facing the rising or setting sun, they close their eyes and spread their arms wide, breathing in the changing light. As the colors shift from darkness to light, or from light to darkness, the practitioner reflects on the balance between creation and dissolution, light and shadow. They feel the warmth of the sun as a physical manifestation of Ahura Mazda's presence, a reminder that the same energy that gives life to stars and galaxies also flows within their own heart.

Through this practice, the practitioner experiences a moment of unity with the cosmos, where the boundaries between the self and the universe dissolve, leaving only the flow of light. It is a powerful way to end or begin the day, grounding the practitioner in the awareness that they are not separate from the world but are a part of its eternal cycle. This state of communion opens the heart to the mysteries of creation, allowing the practitioner to perceive the divine in every moment, every breath, and every movement of the universe.

These advanced practices of Cosmic Consciousness guide the Zoroastrian toward a life of deeper insight, compassion, and connection. By expanding their awareness beyond the individual self, they begin to see the world through the eyes of asha, recognizing the intricate web of relationships that connect all beings. This vision empowers them to live with a sense of purpose and peace, knowing that their journey is part of a grander design, one that spans the stars and reaches into the heart of the divine. In this way, Cosmic Consciousness becomes not just a state of mind, but a way of being—one that celebrates the unity of all life and the endless dance of creation under the guiding light of Ahura Mazda.

Chapter 12
The Role of the Priests

Within the ancient framework of Zoroastrianism, the priests—known as Mobeds—hold a central place, serving as the keepers of sacred traditions and the intermediaries between the spiritual and material worlds. Their role is deeply rooted in the teachings of Zoroaster, whose revelation from Ahura Mazda emphasized the importance of maintaining the divine order of asha through ritual purity, prayer, and the dissemination of spiritual knowledge. The Mobeds embody this mission, preserving the spiritual practices that guide the faithful on their journey towards the Light Divine.

The origins of the Mobeds trace back to the earliest days of Zoroastrian worship, when Zoroaster himself gathered disciples and imparted to them the knowledge of the Avesta, the sacred texts. These disciples became the first custodians of Zoroastrian wisdom, ensuring that the hymns, prayers, and rituals that Zoroaster introduced would be carried forward through time. Over centuries, their role evolved into a formal priesthood, tasked with conducting ceremonies, interpreting sacred texts, and offering guidance to the community. Even today, the Mobeds continue to serve as vital links between the ancient traditions and modern practitioners.

One of the primary responsibilities of the Mobed is to maintain the sacred fires that burn within Zoroastrian temples, known as Atash Behrams or fire temples. These fires, which range from Atash Dadgah (smaller, domestic fires) to the revered Atash Behram (the highest grade of fire), are kept burning continuously as symbols of Ahura Mazda's divine presence. The

Mobed is entrusted with the careful rituals that sustain these flames, ensuring that they remain pure and unpolluted. Each day, they tend the fire, reciting prayers from the Yasna and the Vendidad, feeding it with sandalwood and other sacred offerings.

This act of tending the fire is more than a simple ritual; it is an act of devotion that symbolizes the perpetual struggle to maintain the light of asha in the world. The fire represents truth, purity, and the spiritual light that illuminates the path toward divine wisdom. In caring for this sacred flame, the Mobeds are seen as guardians of spiritual integrity, maintaining a space where the physical world can meet the divine. For the faithful, participating in rituals performed around this sacred fire provides a direct connection to the cosmic energies of Ahura Mazda, reinforcing their own commitment to the principles of truth and righteousness.

Beyond maintaining the sacred fire, the Mobeds play a crucial role in the transmission of Zoroastrian prayers and scriptures. Much of the Avesta—the core body of Zoroastrian holy texts—has been passed down orally through generations of priests. This oral tradition requires not only memorization but a deep understanding of the meanings and nuances behind each verse. A Mobed spends years learning to recite the Avesta with the proper intonations, ensuring that each prayer carries the intended spiritual resonance. This transmission of knowledge is seen as a sacred duty, preserving the words that Zoroaster received from Ahura Mazda so that they remain pure and unaltered through time.

The Mobeds are also responsible for interpreting these sacred texts, providing guidance to the community on how to apply the teachings of the Avesta in their daily lives. This role is particularly important during rites of passage such as births, weddings, and funerals, where the Mobed leads the ceremonies and offers prayers that align with the principles of asha. Their presence during these moments is seen as a way to bless and sanctify significant events in the lives of the faithful, ensuring that each transition is infused with spiritual meaning and aligned with the divine order.

In addition to officiating over life's pivotal moments, the Mobeds guide the faithful through rituals of purification, such as the Kushti and the Nahn. The Kushti ritual, which involves the tying of a sacred girdle made of wool around the waist, is a daily practice that symbolizes the individual's commitment to the Zoroastrian faith. The Mobed teaches the significance of this act, explaining that each knot tied during the recitation of prayers represents a bond to asha and a rejection of druj, the forces of chaos and falsehood. The Nahn, or ritual bath, is another purification rite that is overseen by a Mobed, often before major religious ceremonies or during times of spiritual renewal.

Through these rituals, the Mobeds help practitioners to understand that purification is not only a physical act but a spiritual one. The cleansing of the body is seen as a reflection of the cleansing of the soul, preparing the individual to enter sacred spaces or to engage in prayer with a mind free from distraction and impurity. The Mobed guides the faithful through this process, ensuring that the rituals are performed correctly and that their spiritual significance is fully realized. In this way, the Mobed serves as both a teacher and a facilitator, helping each practitioner to deepen their connection to the divine.

Another aspect of the Mobed's role is to lead community worship during Zoroastrian festivals, such as Nowruz (the Persian New Year) and Gahambars (seasonal festivals that honor the creation of the world). During these celebrations, the Mobed conducts the Jashan ceremony, where prayers are offered to the Yazatas (divine beings) and the Fravashis (spirits of the righteous). The Jashan is a communal event that brings together the Zoroastrian community in a shared act of devotion, reinforcing the bonds of fellowship and reminding everyone of their shared commitment to asha.

The Mobed prepares the sacred offerings for the Jashan, which include fruits, milk, flowers, and incense. As the prayers are recited, the offerings are blessed and shared among the participants, symbolizing the abundance that comes from living in harmony with the divine order. The role of the Mobed in these ceremonies is to act as a channel, directing the community's prayers to Ahura Mazda and inviting the blessings of the spiritual realms into the physical world. For many Zoroastrians, participating in these rituals under the guidance of a Mobed is a deeply moving experience, one that reinforces their sense of belonging to a tradition that stretches back millennia.

In addition to their duties within the temple, Mobeds are often called upon to provide spiritual counseling and support to individuals seeking guidance in their personal lives. This role requires a deep understanding of both the spiritual and practical aspects of the Zoroastrian faith, as the Mobed helps individuals navigate challenges while maintaining their commitment to asha. Whether offering advice on ethical dilemmas, assisting with the interpretation of dreams, or providing comfort during times of grief, the Mobed acts as a spiritual anchor, helping the faithful to find their way through life's complexities with wisdom and compassion.

The training of a Mobed is a rigorous process that combines study, meditation, and the mastery of rituals. Young men who wish to become Mobeds are often trained from a young age, learning the Avesta and the Pahlavi languages, the proper conduct of ceremonies, and the philosophy that underpins the Zoroastrian faith. This training is seen as a spiritual journey in itself, where the initiate gradually deepens their understanding of the divine mysteries and prepares themselves to take on the mantle of spiritual leadership. The process of becoming a Mobed is not merely about acquiring knowledge; it is about embodying the principles of asha so fully that they become a living example of the teachings of Zoroaster.

For the Zoroastrian community, the Mobeds represent a living link to the past, a reminder of the enduring power of the faith that has survived through centuries of change. Their role is not only to preserve ancient practices but to adapt them to the needs of contemporary life, ensuring that the spiritual wisdom of

Zoroaster remains relevant and accessible. Through their dedication, the Mobeds keep the sacred flame of Zoroastrianism burning brightly, offering a light that guides the faithful toward the path of truth, purity, and connection to the Divine Light.

As we delve deeper into the responsibilities and spiritual duties of the Mobeds in Zoroastrianism, it becomes clear that their role extends beyond the mere performance of rituals. The Mobed serves as a bridge between the esoteric teachings of the faith and the daily lives of the community, ensuring that each member can access the spiritual resources they need for their own growth.

One of the key aspects of the Mobed's work is to provide tools for spiritual independence, teaching lay practitioners how to integrate the principles of asha into their everyday routines. While the presence of a Mobed is essential for major ceremonies and complex rites, many aspects of Zoroastrian practice are designed to be carried out individually or within the family unit. The Mobed often instructs families on the proper recitation of daily prayers, such as the Ashem Vohu and the Yatha Ahu Vairyo, which are central to maintaining a personal connection with the divine. These prayers, recited upon waking, before meals, and at the close of the day, help to keep the mind aligned with the truths of asha.

Beyond teaching the prayers, the Mobeds guide practitioners in the performance of simplified versions of key rituals. For instance, while the full Yasna ceremony—a central ritual involving the recitation of sacred hymns and the offering of haoma—requires the presence of a Mobed, many elements of it can be adapted for personal practice. The Mobed might teach individuals how to perform a simple Dastur (blessing ritual) at home, using clean water and fire to purify their living space and invite the blessings of Ahura Mazda. Through these smaller, accessible rites, Zoroastrians are empowered to maintain a sense of spiritual continuity throughout their daily lives, even when they cannot attend temple ceremonies.

A significant part of the Mobed's guidance involves helping practitioners understand the deeper meanings behind the symbols and rituals they perform. For instance, when instructing on the lighting of a home fire for meditation or prayer, the Mobed explains that the flame represents more than physical light—it is a manifestation of Atar, the divine fire that burns away falsehood and reveals the truth. By understanding the spiritual symbolism behind the rituals, practitioners are able to perform them with greater intention and focus, turning each act into a moment of connection with the divine. This emphasis on understanding aligns with the Zoroastrian belief that wisdom (khratu) is a key component of spiritual progress.

In times of need, the Mobeds also provide counsel on how to perform rites for specific purposes, such as protection, healing, or guidance. When a family faces difficulties, such as illness or a period of uncertainty, the Mobed may recommend specific prayers from the Vendidad or suggest a Jashan (a thanksgiving ceremony) to align the family with the energies of renewal and resilience. The Mobed might also advise on how to prepare a space in the home for meditation, emphasizing the importance of cleanliness and the arrangement of sacred items like a small fire, a bowl of water, and a copy of the Avesta to create a sanctuary of peace and divine connection.

This adaptability extends to the way Mobeds assist with modern celebrations of ancient festivals. For example, during Nowruz, the Persian New Year, the Mobed might lead a communal ceremony at the temple, but they also provide families with guidance on how to prepare their own Haft-Seen table—a symbolic arrangement of seven items that represent prosperity, health, and spiritual renewal. By instructing on the meanings of each item, such as sabzeh (sprouts for rebirth) or sekeh (coins for wealth), the Mobed ensures that even those celebrating at home can connect with the spiritual essence of the season. This blending of communal and private worship allows Zoroastrians to feel a part of a larger spiritual tradition while adapting it to the rhythms of their personal lives.

Another important aspect of the Mobed's role is guiding the faithful in the observance of Ratus, the five daily divisions of time that correspond to different spiritual energies. Each division, from Havan (dawn) to Ushahin (night), has specific prayers and meditations associated with it, helping practitioners to align their thoughts and actions with the flow of time as it is sanctified by Ahura Mazda. The Mobed helps the community understand how to integrate these observances into their routines, offering practical advice on how to adapt the prayers to fit into a modern lifestyle. For instance, they might suggest shorter recitations for those with demanding schedules, emphasizing that even a few minutes of focused prayer can maintain the connection to the divine rhythm of the day.

The role of the Mobed also extends to the care of those who are transitioning through life's final stages. When a member of the community passes away, the Mobed performs the Sagdid ritual, where a dog is brought near the body to ensure that the spirit has left, followed by the prayers of the Gathas that guide the soul across the Chinvat Bridge. The Mobed provides comfort and support to the grieving family, explaining the meaning behind each part of the funeral rites, and emphasizing the Zoroastrian belief in the soul's journey toward the light. These teachings help the living find peace, knowing that their loved ones are guided by the divine presence of Ahura Mazda as they move beyond the physical world.

Moreover, the Mobeds play a crucial role in the transmission of ethical teachings, helping the community understand how to apply the moral principles of the faith to contemporary challenges. Through sermons and discussions, they address issues such as honesty in business, the importance of family harmony, and the need for ecological responsibility—a reflection of the Zoroastrian reverence for nature. In doing so, the Mobeds ensure that the teachings of asha remain vibrant and relevant, offering guidance on how to live a life that honors both ancient wisdom and modern realities.

For those unable to attend regular services, Mobeds have also adapted to contemporary forms of communication, offering online sessions and guidance through digital platforms. This modern adaptation allows the teachings of Zoroastrianism to reach practitioners across the world, ensuring that no matter where a Zoroastrian might live, they have access to the spiritual support and teachings of a Mobed. In this way, the Mobed's role continues to evolve, embracing new methods while staying true to the ancient charge of guiding the faithful toward asha.

Finally, the Mobeds remind the community that while they serve as guides, each Zoroastrian is ultimately responsible for their own spiritual journey. The emphasis is on the personal connection with Ahura Mazda, cultivated through daily prayers, ethical actions, and a commitment to the light. The Mobed serves as a mentor, teaching the skills needed to walk this path, but the journey itself is one that each individual must undertake. This approach reflects the Zoroastrian belief in free will and personal responsibility, encouraging each person to be a bearer of light in their own life.

Through their work, the Mobeds help to create a vibrant spiritual community where the teachings of Zoroaster continue to flourish. By offering both the depth of ancient traditions and the flexibility to adapt them to modern life, they ensure that the sacred fire of Zoroastrianism burns brightly, lighting the way for all who seek the path of asha. In this way, the Mobed's role transcends the rituals they perform, embodying the timeless connection between the divine and the human, and guiding each soul toward a deeper understanding of their place within the cosmos.

Chapter 13
The Nowruz Ceremony

In the heart of Zoroastrian tradition, the festival of Nowruz holds a place of profound significance, representing both the renewal of life and the triumph of light over darkness. Nowruz, literally meaning "New Day," marks the beginning of the Zoroastrian New Year, a time when the cosmos itself is believed to realign with the energies of growth and rebirth. This celebration, which coincides with the vernal equinox, invites the faithful to partake in a sacred cycle that reflects the eternal renewal of creation under the guidance of Ahura Mazda.

The roots of Nowruz stretch back over 3,000 years, intertwining with the earliest Zoroastrian practices, where the changing of seasons was seen as a manifestation of Ahura Mazda's divine order (asha). As the earth awakens from the dormancy of winter, so too do the hearts of Zoroastrians open to the possibilities of new beginnings. The festival serves as a reminder of the cosmic struggle between the forces of light and darkness, echoing the Zoroastrian belief that the world is in a constant state of flux, moving towards ultimate perfection and balance.

Central to the observance of Nowruz is the concept of purification—of both the physical and spiritual realms. In the weeks leading up to the festival, Zoroastrian families engage in rituals known as Khaneh Tekani, or "shaking the house." This practice involves cleaning homes from top to bottom, removing dust and old items that represent stagnation. This act of physical cleansing is paralleled by a spiritual purification, where individuals reflect on the past year, seeking to shed negative thoughts and behaviors that may have accumulated. It is believed that just as a clean house invites positive energies, a purified mind and heart create space for divine blessings.

The festival's rituals culminate in the setting of the Haft-Seen table, a central element of the Nowruz celebration. The Haft-Seen, meaning "Seven S's," is an arrangement of seven symbolic items that each begin with the Persian letter س (S). These items—Sabzeh (sprouts), Samanu (sweet pudding), Senjed (dried oleaster fruit), Seer (garlic), Seeb (apple), Somāq (sumac), and Serkeh (vinegar)—are chosen for their representations of life, health, and spiritual virtues. Each element carries a deep meaning: Sabzeh, for instance, symbolizes rebirth and the renewal of nature, while Seer represents the medicine that guards against illness and evil influences.

Beyond these items, the Haft-Seen often includes additional symbols that enrich its spiritual depth. A mirror, placed at the center, reflects the light and reminds participants of the importance of self-reflection and clarity. An egg or goldfish symbolizes fertility and the potential for new life, while a candle is lit as a tribute to the eternal flame of Atar, the sacred fire. Zoroastrians believe that through these symbols, they create a microcosm of the divine order within their homes, inviting the blessings of Ahura Mazda for the year ahead.

On the day of Nowruz itself, Zoroastrians gather with their families to offer prayers and reflections before the Haft-Seen. A key part of the celebration involves the recitation of hymns from the Gathas, the sacred songs of Zoroaster. These ancient verses, rich with spiritual insights, are chanted to invite the presence of the Yazatas (divine beings) and to reaffirm the family's commitment to the path of asha. The Mobed, if present, leads the recitations, but in many homes, the head of the household may also take on this role, guiding the family in a collective act of devotion.

The prayer ceremony is followed by the sharing of a special meal, which includes dishes rich in symbolism and meaning. Foods such as sabzi polo (herbed rice) and fish are served, representing abundance and the fertility of the earth. Sweets like baklava and shirini are shared to signify the sweetness that is hoped to fill the coming year. This communal meal is not only a time for physical nourishment but also for the sharing of stories, wisdom, and blessings among family members. It is a time when the young listen to the tales of their elders, learning the lessons of the past and understanding their place within the continuum of Zoroastrian tradition.

An essential element of Nowruz is the practice of Hajjat, or the giving of gifts and the settling of old debts. This tradition reflects the Zoroastrian values of generosity (Spenta Mainyu) and justice. Elders distribute eidi—gifts of money or sweets—to the younger members of the family, symbolizing their blessings and hopes for prosperity. At the same time, families take this opportunity to resolve conflicts, make amends, and forgive grievances, thus starting the new year with a heart unburdened by past disputes. This focus on reconciliation and generosity underscores the importance of harmony, not only within the family but also with the larger community.

One of the most iconic aspects of Nowruz is the ritual of jumping over fire, known as Chaharshanbe Suri, which occurs on the last Wednesday before the New Year. Participants leap over small bonfires, chanting phrases such as, "Give me your redness, take away my paleness," symbolizing the release of negative energy and the absorption of the fire's purifying warmth. This act, while not exclusive to Zoroastrianism, has deep roots in the ancient reverence for Atar as a purifier and a bridge between the material and spiritual realms. It is a moment of communal joy, where the laughter and cheers of participants fill the air, dispelling the lingering shadows of winter.

Nowruz is more than a celebration; it is a time of profound spiritual alignment, where each act is infused with intention and devotion. As Zoroastrians light the candles on the Haft-Seen and recite the ancient hymns, they renew their commitment to walk the path of truth, to honor the divine order of asha, and to serve as bearers of light in a world that often leans towards darkness. The festival embodies the cyclical nature of life and the eternal return to the light, mirroring the Zoroastrian belief that all creation moves towards a final state of cosmic harmony.

For the faithful, Nowruz serves as a reminder that just as the earth turns towards the sun, so too must the human soul continually turn towards the Light Divine, seeking purification, renewal, and growth. It is a time when the barriers between the physical and spiritual worlds seem to thin, allowing practitioners to feel a closer connection to Ahura Mazda, whose presence is invoked in every symbol, every prayer, and every act of gratitude.

To begin, the preparation for Nowruz is an integral part of the spiritual process, as it symbolizes both physical and metaphysical cleansing. Practitioners are encouraged to start with Khaneh Tekani, the traditional cleaning of the home. This ritual is more than simple tidying; it is a deliberate act of clearing out stagnant energies. Start by sweeping and washing the floors, paying special attention to corners where dust and negative energies might gather. As you clean, recite short prayers like Ashem Vohu or Yatha Ahu Vairyo, inviting the presence of purity and light into each room. Open the windows to allow fresh air to circulate, which is believed to carry away any lingering negativity, making space for the new energies of the coming year.

Next, setting up the Haft-Seen table is a key step in preparing for the Nowruz celebration at home. Choose a place of honor in the living room or a quiet corner where family and guests can gather. Cover the table with a clean white cloth, symbolizing purity and new beginnings. Arrange the seven sacred items—Sabzeh, Samanu, Senjed, Seer, Seeb, Somāq, and Serkeh—with care, making sure to reflect on their deeper meanings as you do so. The intention behind this act is to align your heart and mind with the virtues they represent, such as patience, sweetness, and resilience. Including a mirror on the table is particularly significant, as it serves as a reminder to reflect upon one's own inner state and to seek clarity as the new year begins.

As Nowruz approaches, prepare to light a candle at the center of the Haft-Seen. This candle represents the eternal flame of Atar, the divine fire that burns within every Zoroastrian's soul. When you light it, offer a silent prayer to Ahura Mazda, asking for guidance, protection, and the illumination of your spiritual path. For those with access to a traditional Zoroastrian oil lamp, lighting this sacred flame can be a beautiful way to honor the ancient rituals, but any small candle can serve the purpose if treated with reverence.

The first moments of Nowruz, coinciding with the exact time of the vernal equinox, are filled with spiritual potency. At this time, gather with family members around the Haft-Seen table. If alone, take a moment to center yourself, focusing on the flame as a symbol of your connection to the divine. Recite verses from the Gathas, or choose prayers like the Airyaman Ishya for healing and blessings. If possible, play a recording of traditional Avesta hymns softly in the background, allowing the ancient words to fill your space with their protective and uplifting energies.

As you recite these prayers, visualize the renewal of the world around you—imagine the earth awakening, the flowers blooming, and the sun's warmth returning to the land. This visualization is more than a symbolic act; it is a means of aligning your spirit with the rhythms of nature, tuning into the cycle of life that Nowruz celebrates. Feel the blessings of Ahura Mazda entering your home, filling it with light and peace.

After the prayer and reflection, it is time to share a meal in the spirit of Nowruz. Prepare dishes that hold personal or traditional significance. Rice, especially when cooked with fresh herbs, embodies the growth and prosperity that the new year promises. Fish, with its association with abundance, is another common dish that adorns the Nowruz table. As you eat, take time to express gratitude for the nourishment you have received, and to share stories and hopes for the year to come. This shared meal is an expression of both physical and spiritual sustenance, a time to deepen connections with those around you.

In modern times, not all practitioners have the opportunity to celebrate Nowruz in large community gatherings, but this does not diminish the power of a home-based ceremony. Even those separated by distance can connect spiritually through shared practices. Families spread across different regions may synchronize their Nowruz prayers or exchange photos of their Haft-Seen tables, creating a virtual sense of unity. This adaptability speaks to the enduring nature of Zoroastrianism, which emphasizes the power of intention and devotion over the mere outward form of rituals.

A key aspect of adapting Nowruz for modern life is maintaining its focus on inner transformation. Beyond the physical rituals, practitioners are encouraged to take time for personal reflection during the Nowruz period. Consider journaling about the past year—its challenges, lessons, and the moments of joy that brought growth. Reflect on what aspects of yourself you wish to leave behind with the old year, and what new qualities you hope to cultivate. This practice aligns with the Zoroastrian principle of self-improvement, where each individual is seen as capable of contributing to the cosmic order through their own actions and choices.

In the days following Nowruz, it is traditional to visit loved ones and exchange wishes for the new year, known as Did-o-Bazdid. For those who cannot visit in person, even a phone call or a heartfelt message can carry the same intention of spreading joy and blessings. The act of reaching out to others reinforces the communal aspect of Nowruz, reminding us that our own spiritual renewal is tied to the well-being of those around us. Through these gestures of connection, the energy of Nowruz extends beyond the boundaries of individual homes, weaving a web of light and goodwill throughout the community.

As the Nowruz season comes to a close, many Zoroastrians conclude the celebration with the ritual of Sizdah Bedar, or "getting rid of thirteen." This involves spending the thirteenth day of the new year outdoors, usually in nature, where families gather to picnic and enjoy the elements. At the end of the day, the Sabzeh—the sprouted greens from the Haft-Seen—are cast into a river or stream, symbolizing the release of negativity and the return of life to nature. For those unable to access natural spaces, a small offering of water at home can carry the same spirit, reminding practitioners of their connection to the earth and the importance of gratitude for its gifts.

Through these practices, the essence of Nowruz is preserved, no matter where or how it is celebrated. It serves as a reminder that renewal is a process that begins within, radiating outwards into every aspect of life. Each element of the ceremony, from the prayers to the symbolic meal, offers an opportunity to reconnect with the cycles of the universe and to reaffirm one's place within the divine order of asha. By bringing these traditions into the home, Zoroastrians continue to honor the legacy of their ancestors while adapting their practices to the realities of the modern world.

In every flickering flame, every sprouting Sabzeh, and every heartfelt prayer, the light of Ahura Mazda shines, guiding each soul towards a brighter, more harmonious future.

Chapter 14
The Importance of Prayers

Prayer is the heartbeat of Zoroastrian spirituality, a rhythm that pulses through the daily life of the devout, connecting them to the cosmic order and the presence of Ahura Mazda. In Zoroastrianism, prayer is not simply an act of petition or a ritualized request for blessings; it is an expression of alignment with asha, the universal truth and order that governs all creation. Through prayer, the practitioner opens a channel between the physical and spiritual realms, affirming their commitment to the path of light, wisdom, and righteousness.

The Zoroastrian tradition recognizes the profound power of words, encapsulated in the triadic principle of "Good Thoughts, Good Words, Good Deeds." Words spoken with reverence and intention are believed to have the ability to shape reality, to bring spiritual energies into the material world. Thus, prayers in Zoroastrianism are crafted with great care, each syllable resonating with meaning and purpose. This belief in the creative power of language is rooted in the ancient hymns of the Avesta, particularly in the Gathas, the sacred songs attributed to the prophet Zoroaster himself. These texts are more than scripture; they are the voice of Zoroaster reaching across time, guiding his followers towards the divine.

Central to the daily practice of Zoroastrians are the Yasna and the Khordeh Avesta, collections of prayers that serve various purposes, from personal devotion to community ceremonies. Among these, the Ashem Vohu and Yatha Ahu Vairyo stand as the cornerstones of Zoroastrian prayer life. Simple yet profound, these prayers encapsulate the core teachings of Zoroastrian philosophy and serve as a means to attune the mind and heart to the principles of truth and divine order.

Ashem Vohu is a prayer that celebrates asha, the divine truth. It reads: "Righteousness is the best good. It is radiant; it is desirable. It leads to blessedness." Reciting this prayer is a declaration of the practitioner's desire to live in harmony with the cosmic order, recognizing that righteousness brings both internal peace and alignment with the greater good. When whispered in the quiet hours of dawn or spoken aloud amidst the bustle of daily life, the Ashem Vohu becomes a reminder that the path of truth, though challenging, is the surest route to spiritual fulfillment.

Yatha Ahu Vairyo, another fundamental prayer, speaks of the alignment between the will of the divine and the will of the righteous leader: "As the Lord wills, so the priest, as the will of Mazda, so the works of the righteous for the welfare of the creation." This prayer encapsulates the Zoroastrian understanding that the divine plan and human will can and should be in harmony. The Yatha Ahu Vairyo serves as a call to action, encouraging each individual to align their intentions with those of Ahura Mazda, thereby contributing to the betterment of the world.

The role of these prayers extends beyond their recitation during daily rituals. They serve as spiritual anchors in moments of uncertainty and challenge. Zoroastrians believe that the power of these prayers lies not only in their words but also in the intention behind them. Thus, even when spoken in solitude, they are thought to reach the ears of Ahura Mazda and the divine beings that watch over creation. Each prayer becomes an offering, a way to express gratitude for the blessings of life and to seek guidance through the complexities of existence.

Prayers are woven into the fabric of Zoroastrian life, guiding the faithful from the moment they wake until they retire at night. The daily Farvardin Yasht, a hymn dedicated to the divine spirits, is often recited to seek protection and to honor the spiritual guardians of the family and community. In the morning, Zoroastrians greet the day with prayers that welcome the rising sun, a symbol of the ever-present light of Ahura Mazda. This act of devotion is not merely a routine; it is an acknowledgment of the divine rhythm that underlies the cycle of night and day, and a recognition of the practitioner's role in maintaining the balance between light and darkness.

The midday prayers focus on reinforcing strength and wisdom, often coinciding with the work and responsibilities of daily life. This time is used to recenter, offering thanks for the strength to fulfill one's duties while seeking continued guidance. In the evening, as the sun sets and shadows lengthen, Zoroastrians turn inward with prayers that reflect on the challenges of the day and the hope for a peaceful night. These evening prayers, often whispered in the glow of a sacred flame, serve as a balm for the mind, preparing it for the restful contemplation that sleep brings.

The structure of these daily prayers also highlights the Zoroastrian belief in the interconnectedness of the material and spiritual realms. Just as the sun's journey across the sky marks the passage of time, the regularity of prayer serves as a reminder that each moment carries an opportunity for connection with the divine. By praying at specific times, Zoroastrians align themselves with the natural cycles of the universe, reinforcing their place within the cosmic order.

Beyond personal prayers, Zoroastrianism emphasizes the importance of communal prayer as a means of fostering unity among the faithful. In temples, known as Atash Behram or Agiyari, the presence of the sacred fire provides a focal point for community gatherings. Here, prayers are recited collectively, their echoes filling the space with a palpable sense of shared devotion. The communal aspect of prayer reinforces the idea that the spiritual well-being of the individual is intertwined with that of the community, reflecting the Zoroastrian understanding that each person contributes to the greater harmony of the world.

Even outside the temple walls, the practice of communal prayer continues in family settings. During key life events such as births, marriages, and memorials for the deceased, Zoroastrian prayers are recited to seek blessings, to express gratitude, and to guide the souls of the departed towards the light. These prayers, often passed down through generations, carry with them the wisdom and hope of countless ancestors, linking the present moment to a lineage of faith that stretches back to the time of Zoroaster himself.

For those living in diaspora or far from traditional communities, the daily practice of Zoroastrian prayer becomes a means of maintaining a spiritual connection with their heritage. Through the words of the Avesta, practitioners are able to bridge the distance between themselves and the sacred landscapes of ancient Persia. The prayers, though spoken in different corners of the world, create a shared spiritual space, where the light of Ahura Mazda reaches every heart that turns towards it.

Prayer, in Zoroastrianism, is both an anchor and a guide. It is a way to draw strength in times of adversity and to express gratitude in moments of joy. It is a bridge that spans the gap between the seen and the unseen, offering a path through which the soul can reach out to the divine. Whether whispered in solitude or chanted in the presence of a sacred fire, each prayer is a step towards deeper understanding and a stronger alignment with the path of asha.

The first step in integrating Zoroastrian prayers into daily life is establishing a consistent routine. Zoroastrians traditionally pray five times a day, a practice that aligns the human spirit with the natural cycles of the day. The morning prayer (Havan Gah) welcomes the rising sun, invoking the energy and purity of dawn. Midday prayers (Rapithwin Gah) align with the sun's zenith, a time to seek strength and focus in the heart of the day. As the sun sets, the Uziren Gah serves as a reflection on the day's journey, a moment to offer thanks and seek wisdom. Evening prayers (Aiwisruthrem Gah) prepare the spirit for rest, while the night prayer (Ushahin Gah) offers protection during the hours of darkness, connecting the practitioner to the silence of the cosmos.

To begin each prayer session, it is essential to prepare both the mind and the environment. Find a quiet space, free from distractions, where you can focus your thoughts. Traditional practice suggests facing a source of light—whether it be the rising sun, a sacred fire, or a candle—symbolizing the eternal flame of Ahura Mazda. This act of facing the light is a reminder of the Zoroastrian quest for truth and enlightenment. For those with access to a dedicated prayer space, a small altar can be arranged with symbols of purity, such as fresh flowers, a bowl of water, and the Khordeh Avesta, the book of daily prayers.

Before starting the prayers, take a few moments for Kusti, the ritual act of untying and retying the sacred cord around the waist. This simple ritual serves as a powerful reminder of the covenant between the practitioner and the divine, symbolizing a renewed commitment to the principles of asha. As the Kusti is performed, recite the accompanying prayers with sincerity, focusing on the act of binding oneself to the path of truth and righteousness. With each knot, visualize a connection being made between the physical self and the spiritual realm, a thread that ties the material world to the divine light of Ahura Mazda.

The practice of reciting Ashem Vohu and Yatha Ahu Vairyo can serve as a foundation for every prayer session. Begin by reciting these prayers slowly, allowing each word to resonate within. Focus on the vibration of the sounds, and let the ancient language of the Avesta flow through you. Even for those who do not understand every word of the original text, the intention behind the recitation is key. As you speak these prayers, envision them as a bridge, guiding your spirit closer to the divine light. Repeat each prayer at least three times, as repetition is believed to deepen its spiritual effect, creating a rhythm that calms the mind and opens the heart.

For those who wish to expand their practice, reciting sections of the Khordeh Avesta or the Yasna can bring added depth to prayer sessions. Choose passages that resonate with your personal spiritual needs or the challenges you face. The Ahunavaiti Gatha, for example, offers profound reflections on the nature of creation and the role of humans in the cosmic order. Reciting these hymns with intention can help to anchor the soul during times of uncertainty, providing insight into the greater mysteries of existence.

The use of mantras during prayer is another way to focus the mind and harness the spiritual energy of the words. In Zoroastrianism, mantras like the Yatha Ahu Vairyo are considered to contain potent spiritual power, capable of purifying the environment and the practitioner's inner world. When reciting these mantras, focus on your breath, allowing each exhalation to carry the sound of the mantra outward, like waves spreading across a still lake. With each breath, visualize the mantra's energy expanding, enveloping you in a protective sphere of light. This practice not only strengthens the mind's focus but also serves as a shield against negative influences, creating a sanctuary for the spirit.

The practice of Manthras—sacred chants—also extends to protection and healing. During moments of distress or illness, practitioners can use specific prayers from the Khordeh Avesta, such as the Nirang prayers, which are intended to invoke divine protection and strength. To use these effectively, recite the chosen Nirang while holding a clear intention for what you seek—be it protection, healing, or guidance. This focused intention is thought to direct the energy of the prayer towards its intended purpose, like an arrow finding its mark.

Creating a sacred atmosphere during prayer is equally important. Incense, such as frankincense or sandalwood, can be burned to cleanse the space and invite a sense of calm. The smoke is believed to carry prayers to the higher realms, serving as a tangible connection between the physical world and the spiritual domain. Light a candle or a small oil lamp, representing the eternal flame of Atar, and let its light serve as a reminder of the divine presence that watches over every prayer. These simple acts of devotion, when performed with a clear mind and open heart, can transform any space into a place of spiritual resonance.

For those who seek a deeper connection during prayer, meditative visualization can be a powerful tool. As you recite the words of the prayers, close your eyes and imagine yourself standing before a great, radiant flame—the very embodiment of Ahura Mazda's light. Feel the warmth of this flame on your skin, and let its light fill your entire being, dissolving shadows and fears. Visualize the flame expanding beyond you, illuminating the space around you and spreading outwards, touching the lives of those you hold dear. Through this practice, prayer becomes an act of co-creation with the divine, a way to manifest the light of Ahura Mazda in the world.

In moments of doubt or spiritual dryness, it can be helpful to remind oneself of the power inherent in even the simplest prayers. The act of turning to prayer during these times is itself a testament to the strength of faith, a gesture of trust in the ever-present guidance of Ahura Mazda. Zoroastrianism teaches that the divine is always near, waiting to respond to those who reach out in sincerity. Even when words fail or when the heart feels heavy, the mere act of standing in the presence of the light, repeating a few sacred phrases, can reignite the spark of connection.

For families and small communities, incorporating prayer into shared activities can strengthen bonds and create a sense of unity. Begin gatherings with a collective recitation of Ashem Vohu, allowing each voice to blend into a harmonious whole. Encourage children to learn the simpler prayers, fostering a sense of pride and connection to their heritage. By making prayer a part of everyday interactions, its teachings become a living, breathing part of the home's spirit, shaping the thoughts and actions of each member.

In conclusion, the practice of prayer in Zoroastrianism is a multifaceted journey, one that evolves as the practitioner grows in understanding and spiritual depth. By embracing the rhythms of daily prayer, focusing on intention, and creating a space for divine connection, the practitioner opens a doorway to the Light Divine. Each prayer, whether long or short, becomes a stepping stone towards greater clarity, inner peace, and a closer relationship with Ahura Mazda.

Through these practices, prayer is not merely a ritual to be performed; it becomes a way of life, a continuous dialogue with the divine that nurtures the soul and guides the spirit. The discipline of prayer shapes the heart, aligning it with the eternal principles of asha, and transforms the practitioner into a beacon of the Light Divine. In this way, Zoroastrian prayer holds the power to bring light to every corner of the world, guiding each soul along the path of truth and righteousness.

Chapter 15
Spiritual Forces

In the tapestry of Zoroastrian cosmology, the universe is woven with intricate threads of spiritual forces, entities that exist beyond the material realm yet influence every aspect of life. Among these forces are the Yazatas—beings of light and divine energy who serve as intermediaries between Ahura Mazda and the world. Opposing them are the Daevas, spirits of falsehood and chaos, whose influence seeks to draw humanity away from the path of truth (asha). Understanding the nature of these spiritual beings is crucial for Zoroastrians, as it reveals the dynamics of the cosmic struggle between light and darkness that permeates existence.

The Yazatas, whose name means "worthy of worship," are often likened to angels in other traditions. Each represents a specific aspect of creation or a virtue that mirrors the divine order established by Ahura Mazda. They are not mere personifications of natural forces, but conscious entities that guide and protect those who seek to live in harmony with the divine laws. From the bright rays of Mithra, the guardian of truth and covenant, to Anahita, the celestial water deity who purifies and nourishes, each Yazata plays a role in maintaining the balance and prosperity of the world.

Mithra, perhaps one of the most venerated among the Yazatas, embodies the essence of truth, justice, and the sacred covenant between humanity and the divine. His presence is invoked to ensure the integrity of promises and the fairness of human interactions. In Zoroastrian prayers and rituals, Mithra is often called upon to provide guidance in times of moral uncertainty, his light revealing the true path when choices seem clouded by ambiguity. Through his influence, the faithful are reminded of the importance of honesty and the power of keeping one's word.

Anahita, the spirit of the waters, is another powerful Yazata, representing fertility, healing, and the nurturing aspects of nature. She is often envisioned as a divine figure whose waters cleanse both the physical and spiritual realms. Her role extends beyond the rivers and streams; she is a protector of all life and a source of spiritual renewal. In times of drought or hardship, Zoroastrians may turn to Anahita, offering prayers for her blessings to bring clarity and strength. Her flowing presence is a reminder that, like water, life moves in cycles, and with patience, even the most turbulent currents can bring new beginnings.

Beyond these, there is Sraosha, whose name means "obedience" and who serves as the divine messenger. He listens to the prayers of the faithful and carries them to the realm of the Amesha Spentas and Ahura Mazda. Sraosha is the guardian of rituals, ensuring that each act of devotion reaches its intended purpose. As a protector of the sacred word, he stands against the deception spread by Daevas, guiding the faithful through dreams and intuitions. His presence is subtle, often felt in moments of sudden insight or when the heart resonates with a deeper truth during prayer.

The Daevas, by contrast, are entities that embody chaos, falsehood, and darkness. In the Zoroastrian worldview, they represent the destructive forces that lead humanity away from the path of asha. Unlike the benevolent Yazatas, the Daevas are seen as adversaries to the order established by Ahura Mazda. They thrive in the shadows of ignorance and malice, whispering temptations that lure individuals into actions that disrupt harmony. Each Daeva embodies a different vice or aspect of the destructive spirit (Angra Mainyu), such as envy, deceit, or wrath.

One of the most notorious among the Daevas is Aeshma, the spirit of wrath. He is known for inciting anger and conflict, turning minor disagreements into full-blown disputes. His influence can be seen wherever violence and discord erupt, feeding off the energy of chaos. For Zoroastrians, recognizing the presence of Aeshma means understanding the importance of maintaining inner calm and resolving conflicts through reason and compassion. By invoking the protective presence of Sraosha or Mithra, the faithful can shield themselves from the destructive whispers of Aeshma, choosing peace over fury.

Another significant force among the Daevas is Druj, whose very name means "the lie" or "deception." Druj is not just a single entity but a pervasive force that spreads falsehood, causing confusion and moral disorientation. Her influence is felt when people are led astray by false teachings or when they betray their own principles for short-term gain. The battle against Druj is central to the spiritual struggle in Zoroastrianism, as she represents the antithesis of asha. The recitation of the Ashem Vohu prayer is one of the ways Zoroastrians counteract the influence of Druj, affirming their alignment with truth and purity.

The relationship between the Yazatas and Daevas is not merely one of opposition, but of a dynamic struggle that reflects the choices faced by each individual soul. Within every person exists the potential for both light and darkness, and the actions they take determine which influence will prevail. The Yazatas encourage the cultivation of virtues, guiding the soul towards enlightenment, while the Daevas seek to undermine this progress, leading one into spiritual obscurity. Thus, the spiritual battle is both external, as forces that shape the world, and internal, within the heart of every believer.

This cosmic struggle is not seen as a duality of equals. Zoroastrianism teaches that the power of light is ultimately greater than that of darkness, and that asha will prevail over druj as humanity aligns itself with the teachings of Ahura Mazda. The practice of rituals, prayers, and mindful living are all ways to strengthen the influence of the Yazatas within one's life, creating a spiritual environment where the whispers of the Daevas cannot find purchase.

Understanding the nature of these spiritual forces also provides insight into the role of human beings in the cosmic order. Unlike passive subjects, humans are seen as active participants in the struggle between light and darkness. Every choice, whether a kind word or a harmful act, contributes to the balance of these forces. In this sense, Zoroastrian spirituality places a great emphasis on personal responsibility. The faithful are called to be vigilant, to recognize the influences around them, and to actively align their thoughts and actions with the principles of asha.

The presence of the Yazatas offers a reminder that divine guidance is always accessible to those who seek it. Their energies can be invoked through prayer, meditation, and specific rituals that honor their role in the cosmic order. By calling upon Mithra, a practitioner can seek clarity in difficult decisions; through Anahita, they can find renewal in times of despair. These divine allies serve as beacons, guiding the soul through the complexities of life and helping it navigate the challenges posed by the Daevas.

To begin, invoking the presence of the Yazatas is an act of aligning oneself with the virtues and energies they represent. Each Yazata can be called upon through specific prayers and rituals that resonate with their divine role. For example, to seek truth and clarity in times of uncertainty, one might turn to Mithra. A simple yet powerful invocation can be made by lighting a candle at dawn and reciting the Khorshed Niyayesh, a prayer dedicated to the sun and light. As the flame flickers, focus on the warmth it radiates, imagining that the light of Mithra is dispelling the shadows within the mind, revealing the path of righteousness.

For those in need of healing and renewal, invoking Anahita can bring a sense of peace and restoration. This can be done near a natural body of water, such as a river or a spring, or with a simple bowl of pure water at home. Reciting the Aban Niyayesh, the prayer dedicated to the waters, while gently touching the surface of the water, creates a connection to the purifying essence of Anahita. As you recite, imagine the water absorbing the negative energies and washing away inner impurities, leaving a sense of lightness and clarity. After the prayer, one can sprinkle the water around their space, creating an aura of protection and renewal.

For protection against the harmful influences of the Daevas, the role of Sraosha is paramount. He is the guardian of the rituals and the enforcer of spiritual law. To seek his protection, the recitation of the Srosh Baj, a prayer dedicated to his vigilance, is recommended. This prayer is best recited in the evening, when shadows lengthen and the world becomes more susceptible to the whispers of darkness. As the prayer is spoken, visualize a protective shield forming around you, a barrier of divine light that keeps the deceptive influences of Aeshma and Druj at bay. Feel the presence of Sraosha as a guardian, steadfast and vigilant, guiding you through the silence of the night.

The influence of the Daevas often manifests subtly, through thoughts of envy, anger, or despair that cloud the mind and weaken the spirit. A practical method to counteract these influences is through the recitation of the Ashem Vohu, which is known to realign the soul with the principles of asha. This prayer, short yet potent, is particularly effective when repeated with deep concentration, allowing its rhythm to steady the mind and focus the heart. Reciting the Ashem Vohu three times while focusing on a flame or a clear crystal can amplify its effects, using the purity of the light to cleanse the mind from dark thoughts.

To create a more enduring protection against negative spiritual influences, Zoroastrians may also use nirang, or consecrated prayers that imbue objects with protective power. One such practice involves creating a protective circle with the Kusti, the sacred cord. By tying the Kusti while reciting the Yatha Ahu Vairyo and imagining the sacred threads forming a barrier of light around oneself, the practitioner creates a space where the Daevas cannot enter. This protective circle can be used during meditation, prayer, or before engaging in challenging tasks, providing a spiritual sanctuary where one can connect deeply with the Light Divine.

Another important ritual for invoking the Yazatas and repelling the Daevas is the Atash Niyayesh, a prayer to the sacred fire. This ritual is performed in the presence of a flame, which symbolizes the eternal presence of Ahura Mazda. The fire is seen as a living embodiment of Atar, the spirit of fire, and serves as a bridge between the physical world and the spiritual realms. As the Atash Niyayesh is recited, one can offer sandalwood or incense to the flames, watching as the smoke rises towards the sky, carrying the prayers to the divine. This act of offering to the fire represents a dialogue with the Yazatas, inviting their presence and protection into the sacred space.

In contrast, to banish the presence of Daevas, more active rituals are required. One such ritual involves the use of fumigation with herbs like frankincense, myrrh, and cedar. These sacred herbs are believed to cleanse the environment of negative energies and restore balance. To perform this ritual, light a piece of charcoal and place a small amount of the herbs onto the glowing embers. As the smoke begins to rise, walk through your space, allowing the smoke to fill every corner, while reciting the Yatha Ahu Vairyo or other protective prayers. Visualize the smoke driving away the shadows, leaving behind a space that is filled with the light and peace of the Yazatas.

The act of invoking these spiritual forces and banishing negative influences is not only about external protection; it is also a practice of inner alignment. By consistently calling upon the Yazatas and resisting the Daevas, the practitioner develops a heightened awareness of their own spiritual state. They learn to recognize the subtle shifts in their thoughts and emotions, understanding when they are being led away from the path of asha and when they are moving closer to the Light Divine. This inner vigilance becomes a powerful tool, turning each moment of doubt or temptation into an opportunity for spiritual growth.

Moreover, the relationship with the Yazatas deepens through acts of devotion beyond the formal rituals. Lighting a candle in their honor before a meal, whispering a prayer to Anahita before taking a sip of water, or offering a silent thanks to

Mithra at sunrise—these small acts of recognition cultivate a continuous presence of the divine in everyday life. The Yazatas become not distant figures but close companions, guiding hands that illuminate the path through the world's complexity.

For those who wish to extend this connection beyond themselves, communal rituals can be especially powerful. Gatherings where prayers are recited collectively create a strong spiritual current that can be felt by all present. In such gatherings, the energy of the Yazatas is magnified, creating a shared sense of protection and spiritual upliftment. By coming together in prayer, practitioners not only shield themselves from external darkness but also strengthen the bonds of community, creating a collective light that shines even brighter.

In the end, the rituals and practices that connect the practitioner with the Yazatas and protect against the Daevas are more than ancient traditions; they are living expressions of the cosmic struggle between order and chaos, truth and falsehood. Through these practices, the faithful take an active role in the spiritual battle, aligning their lives with the eternal principles of asha and contributing to the victory of light. Each prayer, each offering, each moment of reflection is a step towards embodying the divine order that Ahura Mazda has set forth.

As the practitioner grows in their understanding and practice of these rituals, they become not just recipients of divine guidance, but participants in the unfolding of the cosmic order. They learn to wield the power of the Yazatas with humility and respect, recognizing that each invocation is a call to be more like the light they seek to invoke. In doing so, they embody the Zoroastrian ideal of being a warrior of the spirit, one who stands firmly in the light, even amidst the shadows of the world.

Chapter 16
The Role of the Family

In the heart of Zoroastrianism lies a profound appreciation for the family as a sacred unit, a cornerstone of spiritual practice, and a bastion against the tides of chaos. The teachings of Zaratustra emphasize that the family is more than a social structure; it is a reflection of the cosmic order, a living manifestation of asha—the divine truth and order that permeates the universe. Within the embrace of family, the Zoroastrian finds not only comfort but also a powerful space for nurturing the virtues of Ahura Mazda and resisting the influences of Angra Mainyu.

The family home, often seen as a microcosm of the larger universe, becomes a sacred space where the daily rituals of Zoroastrian life unfold. It is here that the fire burns, not just in the hearth but in the hearts of those who gather around it, sharing prayers and stories passed down through generations. This flame is a symbol of the ever-present light of Ahura Mazda, whose warmth guides the family in their pursuit of truth, righteousness, and the spiritual principles that underpin their lives.

Central to the family's spiritual role is the concept of Fravashi, the guardian spirit that each individual possesses. When family members come together, their collective Fravashis are believed to create a stronger, unified spiritual force. This unity serves as a shield, protecting against spiritual and physical adversities. Through shared rituals and prayers, such as the Kusti prayers recited each morning and evening, the family binds itself to the cosmic order, creating a sanctuary of light amidst a world often shrouded in darkness.

Within this sacred space, parents assume the role of spiritual guides, tasked with transmitting the teachings of Zaratustra to their children. This transmission is not solely through formal instruction but through the living example set by their daily actions—embodying the principles of Humata, Hukhta, Hvarshta (Good Thoughts, Good Words, Good Deeds). Children learn by observing the reverence with which their parents approach the sacred flame, the respect they show to nature's elements, and the sincerity in their prayers. This living tradition ensures that the essence of Zoroastrian teachings is not lost but rather evolves with each generation, adapting to the challenges of new times while remaining true to its ancient roots.

The practice of regular family prayers is seen as a potent method to strengthen spiritual ties. Families gather before the household altar, often adorned with a simple fire or a lamp, symbolizing the eternal presence of Ahura Mazda. Together, they recite prayers such as the Yatha Ahu Vairyo and Ashem Vohu, aligning their collective will with the cosmic order. These moments of shared devotion create a spiritual bond that transcends the mundane concerns of daily life, reminding each member of their place within a grander scheme, their responsibilities not just to each other but to the entire creation.

Moreover, the celebration of festivals like Nowruz and Mehregan brings a deeper dimension to family life. These festivals serve as a reminder of the cycles of nature and the ever-renewing promise of the Light Divine. During Nowruz, families come together to prepare the Haft-Seen, a symbolic table that represents the renewal of life and the triumph of light over darkness. Each item placed upon the table—sprouts, vinegar, apples, and other symbols—carries a deeper meaning, and their preparation becomes a ritual of connection with the divine. It is a time when the family not only celebrates but also reflects on their journey, their challenges, and the blessings received from Ahura Mazda.

In moments of difficulty, such as illness or grief, the family's spiritual role becomes even more apparent. They turn to the comfort of prayers like the Srosh Baj, seeking the guidance of Sraosha to bring peace to troubled hearts. These practices are not merely about seeking relief; they represent a communal effort to confront suffering with the resilience that comes from faith. The recitation of such prayers together helps to fortify the family's spirit, reminding them that they are not alone in their struggles but are part of a larger spiritual community that spans both the visible and the invisible realms.

Beyond the immediate family, Zoroastrian teachings also extend to the broader community, encouraging families to engage in acts of charity and service. The principle of Spenta Mainyu—the spirit of generosity and creativity—finds expression in how families reach out to support others. It might be through sharing food with those in need, assisting in the upkeep of the local Atash Behram (Fire Temple), or simply offering a comforting presence to a neighbor in distress. These acts are seen not as mere obligations but as extensions of the family's spiritual mission, ways to radiate the light of Ahura Mazda into the wider world.

The connection between family and spirituality is further deepened through the remembrance of ancestors, a practice that keeps the bonds between the living and the departed strong. Zoroastrians believe that the Fravashis of ancestors continue to guide and protect their descendants. During the festival of Farvardigan, families honor these spirits with prayers and offerings, lighting lamps in their memory. This ritual serves as a reminder of the lineage of faith that stretches back through time, linking the living with those who have walked the path of asha before them. It is a moment of profound connection, where the boundaries between the physical and the spiritual grow thin, and the light of the ancestors merges with the flame of the living.

In this way, the Zoroastrian family becomes a custodian of both tradition and spiritual energy. It is within this intimate circle that the larger struggles between light and darkness play out in everyday actions and choices. The home becomes a training ground for virtues, where children learn to choose truth over deceit, kindness over cruelty, and self-discipline over indulgence.

The teachings of Zaratustra remind the family that their collective actions contribute to the larger cosmic battle, and that by nurturing a spirit of harmony and devotion, they align their home with the broader mission of Ahura Mazda.

Yet, this role is not without challenges. Modern life often pulls families in different directions, creating a sense of disconnection from the ancient rhythms that have sustained their ancestors. In this context, the family must find ways to adapt their practices, integrating the timeless rituals of Zoroastrianism into a contemporary lifestyle. It might mean setting aside time for prayers amidst a busy schedule or finding new ways to connect with nature even in urban environments. The resilience of the family lies in its ability to keep the flame of devotion burning, even when external circumstances change.

The family's journey is one of continuous learning and adaptation, but it is also a journey filled with profound rewards. It is within this circle that the beauty of the Zoroastrian path comes alive, not as a distant set of doctrines but as a lived experience that touches every aspect of daily life. Through their dedication to the principles of asha, families find a way to navigate the complexities of existence with grace and purpose, knowing that in each prayer, each act of kindness, and each moment of togetherness, they are contributing to the eternal dance between light and shadow. In doing so, they become not just followers of a faith, but living embodiments of its deepest truths, carriers of the light that Ahura Mazda has entrusted to all who seek the path of righteousness.

To deepen the spiritual life within a Zoroastrian family, there are practices that foster unity and strengthen the connection to Ahura Mazda. These rituals and shared moments of devotion form the bedrock upon which the family builds its spiritual resilience.

Joint prayer sessions serve as one of the most effective means of cultivating spiritual unity within the family. By gathering before a sacred flame or an altar, even in a simple home setting, the family can recite key Zoroastrian prayers such as the

Ashem Vohu and Yatha Ahu Vairyo. These prayers, recited together, create a shared vibration that aligns each member's thoughts with the principles of asha, or cosmic truth. It's not just about the words spoken, but the intention behind them—each utterance becomes a thread that weaves a spiritual tapestry, enveloping the home in an aura of peace and protection.

For families with young children, incorporating rituals into everyday life can take on a simpler, more engaging form. Parents can introduce the significance of the sacred elements—fire, water, earth, and air—through small, interactive rituals. Lighting a candle each evening while explaining that the flame symbolizes Ahura Mazda's eternal light helps children understand the divine presence in tangible ways. As they grow older, these simple acts can evolve into more profound practices, such as learning to recite prayers on their own or helping to tend to the home's sacred space.

Family rituals also extend to mealtime, where prayers of gratitude can be offered before eating. A traditional grace or blessing, expressing thanks for the sustenance provided by Ahura Mazda, becomes an opportunity to instill appreciation for the gifts of life. This simple act ties the physical nourishment of food to the spiritual nourishment of divine connection, reminding each member that their lives are intertwined with the cycles of nature and the blessings of the divine.

During special times of the year, such as the observance of Nowruz or Mehregan, the family can come together to prepare for and participate in more elaborate rituals. Preparing the Haft-Seen table for Nowruz, for instance, becomes a family activity that deepens their connection to the symbolism of renewal and the triumph of light over darkness. Each item placed on the table—sprouts, garlic, vinegar, and more—carries a deep spiritual meaning, and children can be taught the significance behind each. The act of setting up this sacred space, while sharing stories of past celebrations, creates a sense of continuity that ties the family's present to the memories of ancestors.

Moreover, Zoroastrian teachings emphasize the importance of including children in more active roles during rituals, such as helping to maintain the household fire or offering prayers at the altar. This active participation allows them to feel a sense of responsibility and connection to their heritage. When a child lights a lamp before reciting a prayer, they engage not just in a routine but in a living connection with the Light Divine, understanding their role as both a keeper of tradition and a participant in a timeless spiritual journey.

Rituals of remembrance are another key aspect of family spirituality. During Farvardigan, the days dedicated to honoring the Fravashis of departed souls, families can gather to recite prayers for the ancestors, light lamps, and offer food in their memory. This practice serves as a way to maintain the spiritual connection between generations, ensuring that the wisdom and blessings of those who have passed continue to influence and guide the living. Through these acts, children learn to appreciate their lineage and understand that they are part of a continuum that extends beyond the present moment.

In times of hardship, Zoroastrian families can turn to collective prayer as a source of strength. When facing illness, grief, or uncertainty, gathering together to recite the Srosh Baj or other prayers of protection can fortify the family's resilience. The presence of a shared intention during these prayers—each voice rising together in a plea for guidance or healing—creates a profound energy that envelops the home. It is in these moments that the true power of family unity in the Zoroastrian tradition is revealed, showing how the light of Ahura Mazda can shine even in the darkest times.

As children grow older, they can be encouraged to take on more personal spiritual practices, such as daily meditations or deeper study of Zoroastrian texts. Families can set aside time for reading from the Gathas—the hymns of Zaratustra—and discussing their meanings. This communal study session can become a cherished family tradition, where each member shares their interpretations and reflections on the teachings. This not only deepens individual understanding but also fosters a shared exploration of spiritual truths, creating a dialogue that keeps the teachings of Zaratustra vibrant and relevant in the modern context.

Furthermore, the role of parents extends beyond mere instruction; they serve as living examples of how Zoroastrian principles can guide everyday decisions. By demonstrating integrity in their actions, kindness in their speech, and mindfulness in their thoughts, parents model the core values of Humata, Hukhta, Hvarshta. Children, witnessing this alignment between belief and action, learn that their spiritual path is not confined to rituals but extends into every interaction and choice they make.

Incorporating acts of charity into the family's routine is another powerful way to live out the teachings of Spenta Mainyu—the spirit of generosity. Parents can involve their children in community service projects, such as helping those in need or participating in environmental cleanups. These activities become practical expressions of the Zoroastrian commitment to asha, showing that service to others is a form of worship, a way of bringing the light of Ahura Mazda into the world. Through these experiences, children learn the value of selflessness and the joy that comes from helping others.

To maintain a vibrant spiritual life within the family, Zoroastrian households are also encouraged to create spaces that are conducive to meditation and reflection. This might include a small altar where incense can be burned and a candle lit, offering a place where family members can retreat for moments of personal prayer. In this space, the family can also hold group meditations, focusing on visualizing the Divine Light or sending blessings to those in need. These practices help to cultivate a sense of inner calm and connection, reinforcing the family's role as a bastion of spiritual peace amidst the challenges of everyday life.

Lastly, in today's fast-paced world, families may find it challenging to maintain these practices consistently. Yet,

Zoroastrian teachings remind them that even the smallest efforts—such as a short prayer before a meal or a moment of silence together at the end of the day—can hold profound spiritual significance. The key lies in the intention behind these acts, the sincere desire to honor the presence of Ahura Mazda in their lives. With patience and commitment, families can weave these practices into their routines, creating a rhythm that nurtures both their individual and collective spirits.

The journey of a Zoroastrian family is a beautiful tapestry woven with threads of devotion, tradition, and love. Each shared prayer, each ritual performed together, becomes a thread that binds them closer to each other and to the divine. Through these practices, families find that their home is not just a physical space but a living temple, where the sacred light of Ahura Mazda burns brightly, guiding them through life's many twists and turns. It is within this sanctuary that they discover the true essence of their faith—a faith that lives, breathes, and shines through the everyday moments of connection, love, and shared devotion.

Chapter 17
Zoroastrian Ethics

Zoroastrian ethics are a cornerstone of the spiritual life that shapes the thoughts, words, and actions of its followers. Rooted in the fundamental triad of Humata, Hukhta, and Hvarshta—Good Thoughts, Good Words, and Good Deeds—these principles guide the way practitioners interact with the world and the divine. Each aspect of this triad serves as a path toward living in alignment with asha, the cosmic order and truth that Ahura Mazda embodies.

The concept of Humata—Good Thoughts—is more than merely thinking positive thoughts; it calls for a disciplined mind, one that constantly seeks alignment with truth and clarity. Zoroastrian teachings encourage followers to cultivate mindfulness, to become aware of their inner dialogues and the intentions that shape their thoughts. By focusing on clarity and purity in thought, a practitioner begins to align their inner world with the divine order. This means letting go of negative emotions like envy, anger, and deceit, which cloud judgment and distance the soul from its divine potential.

Hukhta, or Good Words, extends the principle of inner purity into the realm of communication. Words, according to Zoroastrian belief, hold a powerful creative energy. When spoken with intention, words can uplift, heal, and strengthen the spirit, not just of the speaker but also of those who hear them. Conversely, words spoken with ill intent or falsehood can lead to spiritual harm and discord. Zoroastrians are taught to speak with integrity, using their words to foster understanding and harmony. In daily life, this might manifest in simple but profound ways—

speaking kindly to strangers, offering encouragement to those in distress, or choosing to remain silent rather than engage in gossip. This mindful use of language is seen as a form of worship, a way to honor the divine spark within each person.

The third pillar, Hvarshta—Good Deeds—represents the tangible actions that reflect the internal virtues of Humata and Hukhta. It is through deeds that thoughts and words find their ultimate expression. In Zoroastrianism, a life of good deeds is not about grand gestures, but about the consistent, everyday acts of kindness and justice that build a just and harmonious world. It means helping those in need, protecting nature, and standing up for truth, even when it is difficult. Through these actions, practitioners become living embodiments of asha, working to bring balance and order into their communities.

The triad of Humata, Hukhta, Hvarshta serves as a framework that integrates spiritual aspirations with practical life. It provides a compass for navigating moral dilemmas, reminding practitioners that their thoughts, words, and actions should always seek to bring about the greatest good. This framework emphasizes the belief in free will—a central tenet of Zoroastrianism. Each individual has the power to choose their path, and through these choices, they align themselves either with the forces of light and order or with the chaos of Angra Mainyu.

In Zoroastrian thought, the commitment to these principles extends beyond personal morality; it carries a cosmic significance. Each act of goodness contributes to the ongoing struggle between the forces of light and darkness, an eternal battle that unfolds not only in the world but within each person's soul. Ahura Mazda, as the supreme creator, endowed humanity with the ability to choose—an ability that defines the essence of the human experience. By choosing Humata, Hukhta, Hvarshta, practitioners actively participate in the divine plan, helping to tip the scales in favor of light, truth, and order.

This ethical framework also has profound implications for the Zoroastrian view of community and society. The emphasis on truth and justice extends to how individuals interact with each other within their families, communities, and broader society. Acts of charity, fairness in business dealings, and the protection of the vulnerable are seen as direct reflections of a person's commitment to asha. Zoroastrian ethics thus promote a vision of society where individuals are not isolated but are interconnected, their actions resonating through the web of relationships that make up the fabric of life.

For the Zoroastrian, ethics are not merely rules to be followed but are pathways to spiritual growth. Each moment of ethical decision-making is an opportunity to strengthen the bond with Ahura Mazda. When faced with a moral challenge, the Zoroastrian is encouraged to turn inward, reflect on the principles of Humata, Hukhta, Hvarshta, and ask themselves how their choice will contribute to the world's harmony. This introspection is itself a form of meditation, a way of aligning the heart with the eternal light that flows from Ahura Mazda.

Yet, living according to these high ideals is not without its challenges. The modern world, with its complexities and distractions, can make it difficult to maintain a constant awareness of one's thoughts, words, and actions. Zoroastrian ethics recognize these struggles, emphasizing that the journey toward asha is one of gradual progress. Perfection is not expected; rather, it is the effort to strive toward these ideals that holds spiritual value. Each effort to correct a harmful thought, to speak a kind word, or to act justly in a difficult situation is seen as a victory in the ongoing spiritual struggle.

The ethics of Zoroastrianism also speak to the relationship between humans and the natural world. Just as Humata, Hukhta, Hvarshta guide human interactions, they also direct how followers interact with the environment. The Earth is viewed as a sacred creation of Ahura Mazda, and therefore, actions that harm the natural world are seen as offenses against asha. Ethical living thus includes environmental stewardship, such as the protection of clean water, the planting of trees, and the respectful treatment of all living beings. Through these acts, Zoroastrians fulfill their role as custodians of creation, helping to preserve the divine order in the natural world.

In the Zoroastrian vision, a life lived according to these principles brings the soul closer to its divine origin. It is believed that when a person practices Humata, Hukhta, Hvarshta consistently, they become a vessel through which the Light Divine can flow more freely. This is not only beneficial in the spiritual realm but also creates a life of fulfillment and inner peace. Aligning one's life with these principles fosters a sense of purpose, a recognition that each action—no matter how small—has the potential to contribute to a greater cosmic harmony.

As the practitioner navigates through the complexities of life, Zoroastrian ethics serve as a guiding star, pointing toward a path of inner and outer harmony. These principles remind each person that the divine light resides within them, waiting to be expressed through their thoughts, their words, and their deeds. And in this way, the journey of a Zoroastrian is not just a personal quest for spiritual purity but a contribution to the eternal struggle for the triumph of light, truth, and order in the universe.

With the foundation of Humata, Hukhta, Hvarshta—Good Thoughts, Good Words, and Good Deeds—clearly established, the next step for a Zoroastrian practitioner is to integrate these principles deeply into daily life. This process is not merely a matter of following guidelines; it is a spiritual practice, a transformative path that aligns the soul with the cosmic order of asha. By focusing on practical methods to embody these ideals, one begins to see how each choice contributes to a life illuminated by the Light Divine.

One effective approach to cultivating Humata in everyday life is through regular self-reflection. At the end of each day, a practitioner may take time to review their thoughts and actions, asking themselves whether they were guided by truth and clarity. Did they allow negative thoughts to take root, or did they seek to replace them with more constructive perspectives? This practice is akin to a mental inventory, where one identifies the influences that draw them away from the path of light. In doing so, practitioners can consciously redirect their minds toward compassion, honesty, and the pursuit of wisdom. Over time, this daily practice becomes a form of meditation, gradually purifying the mind and aligning it more closely with the Light Divine.

To incorporate Hukhta, the principle of Good Words, into daily interactions, one might begin by choosing specific moments to practice mindful speech. For example, before engaging in conversations that may carry a significant emotional weight, like discussions with family members or difficult work situations, a Zoroastrian may take a few moments to breathe and align their words with truth and kindness. A simple prayer or silent invocation of Ahura Mazda's guidance can serve as a reminder that words are not just tools for communication but vessels of spiritual energy. This awareness helps transform conversations into opportunities for healing and connection, even when discussing challenging topics.

Another practice involves reciting traditional Zoroastrian prayers or mantras, such as the Ashem Vohu, before beginning the day. The rhythmic recitation of these sacred words reinforces the principle of Hukhta, allowing the mind and heart to harmonize with the vibrations of truth. The daily repetition of these prayers not only strengthens one's connection to Ahura Mazda but also cultivates a habit of speaking with sincerity and compassion throughout the day. As these practices become ingrained, they extend naturally into interactions with friends, family, and even strangers, allowing the practitioner to become a source of light and peace in their community.

The embodiment of Hvarshta, Good Deeds, can be seen in both small acts of kindness and in more deliberate efforts to serve others. Zoroastrians might set aside time each week for charitable actions, such as volunteering in community activities, supporting those in need, or simply offering help to a neighbor. These actions, though seemingly ordinary, are seen as offerings to Ahura Mazda, a way of manifesting divine will in the material world. Such deeds create ripples in the spiritual realm, contributing to the triumph of light over darkness in both personal and cosmic battles. By engaging in acts of service, practitioners become active participants in the divine drama that Zoroastrianism envisions, where every good deed strengthens the fabric of asha.

A practical method to deepen one's commitment to Hvarshta is through the concept of Dana—the act of giving. In Zoroastrian teachings, Dana is more than just material generosity; it is an expression of one's spiritual abundance. Practitioners are encouraged to give without expectation, offering not only material resources but also time, knowledge, and support. This practice can take many forms, such as mentoring younger members of the community, sharing spiritual insights with those who seek understanding, or even dedicating a portion of daily prayer for the well-being of others. Through these acts, the practitioner strengthens their bond with the community and deepens their own spiritual path.

Balancing these three principles requires a sense of self-discipline and awareness. It is not uncommon for practitioners to encounter situations where maintaining the balance between thought, word, and deed becomes challenging—where thoughts of doubt arise, words fail to carry their intended meaning, or actions do not align with spiritual ideals. In these moments, Zoroastrian teachings encourage turning to the practice of Patet, or repentance. Patet involves acknowledging one's mistakes, seeking forgiveness from Ahura Mazda, and resolving to correct one's path. It is a reminder that the journey toward asha is a dynamic process, one that allows for growth through learning from one's imperfections.

As part of this process, maintaining a journal of ethical reflections can be especially beneficial. This practice involves writing down moments where one felt aligned with Humata, Hukhta, Hvarshta, as well as those where challenges were faced. By documenting these experiences, the practitioner creates a personal record of their spiritual progress, which serves as both a mirror and a guide. This journal can become a valuable tool for self-accountability, providing insights into recurring patterns and offering a means to celebrate successes along the path.

An essential aspect of integrating Zoroastrian ethics into daily life is understanding the interconnectedness between personal growth and the well-being of the world. Each time a practitioner makes a conscious choice to align with asha, they are contributing to the greater cosmic balance. This perspective fosters a deep sense of responsibility, not only to oneself but to all beings. It encourages actions that are mindful of their impact on the environment, community, and future generations. Planting a tree, conserving water, or choosing to reduce waste can be seen as expressions of Hvarshta—ways of serving the Earth, which Zoroastrians believe is a sacred creation of Ahura Mazda.

Through these practices, Zoroastrians are reminded that the path to spiritual alignment is not a solitary endeavor but one that is lived through relationships—with oneself, with others, and with the divine. The discipline of Humata, Hukhta, Hvarshta encourages constant growth and self-refinement, recognizing that each moment is an opportunity to deepen the connection to the Light Divine. It is this ongoing process of striving for ethical alignment that transforms everyday life into a sacred journey.

Ultimately, living by Zoroastrian ethics is a commitment to the light within and a pledge to let that light shine through every aspect of existence. It calls for courage—to confront one's own shadows and to stand firm in the face of falsehood. It asks for compassion—to see the divine in every person and to respond with kindness. And above all, it demands faith—faith in the goodness of the universe, faith in the power of truth, and faith in the potential of each soul to become a beacon of the Light Divine. This is the promise of Zoroastrian ethics: a life that is not merely lived, but one that shines as an offering to the eternal flame of Ahura Mazda.

Chapter 18
The Use of Mantras

The resonance of sacred sound has been a cornerstone in many spiritual traditions, and in Zoroastrianism, mantras hold a special place as conduits of divine energy. These chants, recited with devotion and intention, are believed to connect the practitioner to the essence of Ahura Mazda and to channel the power of the Light Divine into their lives. Understanding the origin, purpose, and power of these mantras reveals how words, imbued with spiritual significance, can become tools of transformation.

Mantras in Zoroastrian practice are not simply prayers; they are seen as vibrational patterns that align the speaker with the divine order, or asha. Each recitation is a way to harmonize one's thoughts and intentions with the universal flow of creation. Among the most revered mantras are the Ashem Vohu and the Yatha Ahu Vairyo, whose ancient words have been passed down through generations. These mantras are considered foundational to Zoroastrian worship, carrying with them the wisdom and power of the faith's earliest teachings.

The Ashem Vohu is perhaps the most frequently recited mantra in Zoroastrianism. Its meaning centers on the concept of asha, truth, and the order of the cosmos. The mantra can be translated as: "Righteousness is the best good. It is radiant, it is glorious. Happiness comes to the one who is righteous, for the sake of the highest righteousness." Each word is believed to carry a vibration that purifies the mind and the surroundings. Reciting the Ashem Vohu is a way to focus one's consciousness on truth and to invite the Light Divine into every action. It is often used at the beginning of prayers and rituals, setting a tone of spiritual alignment.

Another vital mantra, the Yatha Ahu Vairyo, serves as a declaration of divine purpose. It translates as: "Just as a leader acts with righteousness, so should we act with righteousness in service. This is the wish of Ahura Mazda." This mantra is traditionally recited during daily prayers and is often used in rituals that seek to draw on divine wisdom and guidance. Its rhythm is intended to attune the practitioner to the will of Ahura Mazda, reminding them of their role as a servant of the divine order. The repetition of these words is thought to create a spiritual current that supports the practitioner in aligning their life with the higher truths of Zoroastrian teachings.

In addition to these core mantras, there are many others used for specific purposes—each tailored to different aspects of spiritual and material life. For example, mantras may be recited to invoke protection, to seek healing, or to cultivate peace in the household. The Kem Na Mazda, a prayer asking for protection from harmful influences, is a powerful tool against negative energies. Its recitation is considered a shield, calling upon Ahura Mazda's guidance and the protection of the Amesha Spentas. Practitioners use it in moments of vulnerability, such as during travel or when facing difficult challenges, to fortify their connection to the divine.

Understanding the significance of each mantra goes beyond its literal meaning. The power of a mantra is believed to lie in its sound, rhythm, and the intention behind its recitation. The sacred vibrations created by the spoken word are thought to resonate with the spiritual planes, allowing the practitioner to access energies that support healing, clarity, and protection. Reciting a mantra, therefore, is not merely a linguistic exercise—it is a meditative practice that unites mind, voice, and spirit. This unity, achieved through repetition and focus, can lead to profound shifts in consciousness.

The practice of mantra recitation is often accompanied by specific rituals to enhance its effects. For instance, many

Zoroastrians light a candle or incense before beginning their recitation, symbolizing the presence of the Light Divine. The act of focusing on the flame while chanting can help to concentrate the mind, turning the recitation into a deeply immersive experience. Some practitioners hold a prayer cord, known as the kusti, in their hands as they chant, using it as a tactile anchor to maintain focus. This physical connection reinforces the spiritual intentions of the mantra, grounding the energy of the recitation into the physical realm.

It is also important to recognize the role of breath in the practice of mantras. Zoroastrian spiritual teachings emphasize the use of breath to control the flow of energy within the body, and this extends to the rhythm of mantra recitation. By coordinating breath with the cadence of the words, practitioners can deepen their state of meditation. This rhythmic breathing, combined with the sacred syllables, is believed to amplify the potency of the mantra, making the recitation not just a prayer but a channel for divine energy.

For those new to the practice, starting with a few simple recitations of the Ashem Vohu or the Yatha Ahu Vairyo each morning can create a foundation for more complex practices. The key is consistency. Daily recitation, even in small amounts, creates a rhythm that integrates the energy of the mantra into one's life. As practitioners become more familiar with the effects of these words, they may choose to extend their practice, exploring longer sessions or incorporating additional mantras into their routine.

Beyond the individual, the communal recitation of mantras also holds great significance in Zoroastrian tradition. Gathering with others to chant creates a collective energy that can elevate the spiritual atmosphere of a space. Whether within the home or at a fire temple, the power of many voices united in prayer is seen as a force that can dispel negativity and invite blessings. This practice emphasizes the communal nature of Zoroastrian spirituality, where the act of coming together in worship reinforces the bonds between individuals and their shared connection to the divine.

The true essence of Zoroastrian mantras lies in their ability to bring the practitioner closer to the Light Divine. Each recitation is a step on the path toward a deeper understanding of Ahura Mazda's will, a means of aligning oneself with the cosmic order. The sounds of these mantras become a bridge between the physical and the spiritual, a way to transcend the limitations of the material world and touch the eternal. Through this practice, the practitioner not only experiences moments of peace and clarity but also contributes to the greater flow of spiritual light within the world.

In the quiet hours of dawn or the stillness of night, when the world seems to pause, the sound of a mantra carries through the air like a whisper of ancient wisdom. It is in these moments that the practitioner can feel the true power of the spoken word—how each vibration, each breath, is a prayer reaching out to the farthest reaches of the cosmos, calling for the blessings of Ahura Mazda. In these moments, the seeker becomes both the voice and the echo, a vessel for the sacred sound that guides the soul toward the eternal flame.

One of the most critical aspects of mantra practice is the understanding of rhythm and intonation. Unlike ordinary speech, mantras are intoned in a specific cadence that resonates with both the physical and spiritual realms. This rhythmic recitation allows the sound to become a form of meditation in itself, each repetition deepening the practitioner's connection to the divine. In the Zoroastrian tradition, mastering the flow of the Ashem Vohu or Yatha Ahu Vairyo involves paying attention to the rise and fall of each syllable, allowing the vibrations to synchronize with the breath.

For beginners, starting slowly and focusing on clarity can help build a strong foundation. Enunciating each syllable with intention ensures that the mantra's vibrations are correctly formed, which is believed to enhance its spiritual potency. This meticulous approach is particularly important in Zoroastrianism, where the purity of sound is seen as a reflection of the purity of thought and spirit. As one becomes more familiar with the mantras, the pace can gradually increase, allowing for a more fluid and natural rhythm that aligns with the practitioner's breathing.

To deepen the practice, practitioners can incorporate the use of breath control, or pranayama, into their mantra recitation. By coordinating the inhalation and exhalation with the phrases, the recitation becomes a cyclical flow of energy. For example, taking a deep breath before beginning the Ashem Vohu, then slowly releasing the breath as each word is spoken, helps to maintain focus and prolong the vibrations. This technique not only enhances concentration but also aligns the energy centers within the body, facilitating a greater flow of spiritual energy.

Visualization is another powerful tool that can be used alongside mantra practice. As the words are spoken, the practitioner might visualize a stream of light emanating from their heart or third eye, extending toward Ahura Mazda. This light, growing brighter with each recitation, represents the bond between the soul and the divine. Such visualization can turn the act of chanting into a deeply immersive experience, where the mantra becomes a bridge between the earthly self and the spiritual realm. This method is especially effective during longer sessions of meditation, where the mind can fully immerse itself in the imagery and energy of the practice.

The environment where mantras are recited also plays a significant role in their effectiveness. A quiet, clean space, preferably one with a small altar or a lit candle, can enhance the atmosphere for spiritual practice. The presence of fire, even in the form of a candle, symbolizes the presence of Ahura Mazda and the Light Divine, offering a focus point for the mind during chanting. Incense, such as sandalwood or frankincense, can also be used to purify the space and elevate the spiritual ambiance, creating a setting where the sacred sounds of the mantra can resonate freely.

For those seeking specific outcomes from their practice, different mantras can be chosen to align with their intentions. For example, in times of emotional turbulence, the Kem Na Mazda serves as a shield, offering protection and calming the mind. In contrast, the Yatha Ahu Vairyo can be used when seeking clarity in decision-making or guidance from Ahura Mazda, as its words focus on aligning one's actions with divine will. By selecting a mantra that matches the desired energy, the practitioner can focus their spiritual work more effectively, transforming the recitation into a targeted practice.

Incorporating mantras into daily life does not necessarily require lengthy sessions; even a few minutes each morning and evening can create a powerful spiritual habit. The morning recitation can serve as a way to set the tone for the day, infusing it with a sense of purpose and alignment with the Light Divine. Evening recitations, on the other hand, can offer a moment of reflection, allowing the practitioner to release the stresses of the day and re-establish their connection with the divine before rest. These daily practices, though simple, build a rhythm that naturally integrates spiritual awareness into all aspects of life.

Group chanting is another dimension of mantra practice that amplifies its effects. When mantras are recited in a community, the collective intention and voices create a powerful current of spiritual energy. This can be experienced in Zoroastrian fire temples during communal prayers, where the resonance of many voices fills the sacred space, creating a palpable presence of the divine. For those who do not have access to a community, even gathering with a few like-minded individuals for joint recitation can have a profound effect, weaving a stronger connection between all participants and the spiritual energies they invoke.

An important aspect of advanced mantra practice is the deepening awareness of subtle shifts in consciousness during recitation. As one progresses, there may come moments when the words seem to fade into the background, leaving a profound stillness in their place. These are moments when the practitioner becomes fully attuned to the vibrations, and the mind reaches a state of quiet focus. In Zoroastrian teachings, these states are considered times when the veil between the physical and spiritual worlds thins, and the presence of Ahura Mazda can be most deeply felt. Recognizing and embracing these moments without clinging to them is key, allowing the spiritual experience to unfold naturally.

To enhance their mantra practice, some practitioners create personal rituals around their recitation. This might involve beginning with a simple prayer of intention, stating the purpose of the session—be it healing, guidance, or gratitude. By framing the practice with an intention, the energy of the mantra becomes directed, focusing the mind and spirit on a particular goal. Ending each session with a moment of silence is also recommended, allowing the vibrations of the mantra to settle into the body and the space. This final moment of stillness can be a time to offer a silent prayer of thanks, acknowledging the presence of the divine that the practice has invoked.

While each practitioner may find their unique rhythm and methods, the essence of mantra practice in Zoroastrianism remains the same: it is a dialogue with the divine, a way to align one's heart, mind, and spirit with the cosmic order of asha. Through consistent practice, mantras become more than words—they become currents of energy, guiding the practitioner through the challenges of life and toward the eternal light. The power of this practice lies in its simplicity, requiring no elaborate preparation but only the sincerity of heart and a willingness to connect.

As one delves deeper into the art of mantra recitation, the sounds become like footsteps on a path, guiding the soul closer to the divine presence of Ahura Mazda. In the echo of each word, the practitioner may find not only a reflection of their inner world but also the whisper of something far greater—a timeless connection to the wisdom of Zaratustra, to the sacred fire that has burned through the ages, and to the light that continues to shine, within and beyond.

Chapter 19
The Vision of Life After Death

Within the intricate cosmology of Zoroastrianism, the journey of the soul after death holds a profound significance. Unlike many other spiritual traditions, the Zoroastrian concept of the afterlife is closely tied to the individual's moral choices during their lifetime.

The Zoroastrian belief in the afterlife centers on the crossing of the Chinvat Bridge, a symbolic passage that every soul must traverse after death. According to ancient teachings, the bridge acts as a threshold between the physical world and the spiritual realm, where the true nature of one's actions, thoughts, and words is revealed. As the soul approaches the Chinvat Bridge, it is confronted with the culmination of its deeds—a profound moment where every action, whether virtuous or malevolent, is weighed. This is not merely a judgment by divine decree but a reflection of the cosmic order, as the universe aligns with the principles of asha (truth) and druj (falsehood).

The bridge is said to transform in size and shape according to the moral weight of the soul's life. For those who have lived a life in harmony with asha, embodying the virtues of truth, compassion, and service, the Chinvat Bridge widens, becoming a clear and welcoming path toward the realms of light. For others, burdened by selfishness and falsehood, the bridge narrows to a razor-thin edge, making the crossing perilous and leading the soul to a darker destination. This dual nature of the bridge embodies the Zoroastrian understanding of justice—where every action has a consequence, and the path to the afterlife reflects the true essence of one's earthly journey.

At the end of this crossing lies the spiritual judgment. Here, the soul meets its daena, a spiritual entity representing the sum of its deeds, thoughts, and words during its earthly existence. For the righteous, this encounter is like meeting a radiant figure, a being that embodies the light they cultivated through virtuous living. For those whose lives were dominated by deceit and harmful actions, the daena appears as a dark and fearsome presence, embodying the shadow they have cast upon the world. This encounter is deeply personal and acts as a mirror, showing the soul the unfiltered reality of its existence.

After this moment of reckoning, the soul is guided to its respective realm. Those who have lived in accordance with asha find themselves welcomed into the House of Song, a realm of light and peace, where they join Ahura Mazda and the Amesha Spentas in a state of divine harmony. It is described as a place where the soul experiences the ultimate connection with the Light Divine, surrounded by an atmosphere of celestial music and spiritual joy. This realm is not simply a reward; it is a natural continuation of the soul's alignment with the cosmic order, a return to the light it has sought throughout its life.

Conversely, souls that are weighed down by druj, who have chosen paths of destruction, deceit, and self-centeredness, are led to the House of Lies. Here, they experience the isolation and suffering that arises from being disconnected from the Light Divine. It is a realm where the darkness they fostered during their life surrounds them, a place of spiritual stagnation where they face the consequences of their choices. Yet, even in this state, Zoroastrianism holds to a belief in eventual redemption. The suffering in the House of Lies is not eternal damnation but a period of purification, an opportunity for the soul to confront its errors and eventually find its way back to the Light Divine.

Central to the Zoroastrian vision of the afterlife is the concept of Frashokereti, the ultimate renewal of the world. This future event represents the final triumph of asha over druj, where all souls, even those that once dwelled in darkness, are eventually purified and reunited with the Light. Ahura Mazda, in collaboration with the righteous forces, brings forth this renewal, transforming existence into a perfect state of harmony. In this new world, pain and suffering are dissolved, the shadows of Angra Mainyu are banished, and the universe is restored to its original, unblemished form.

The anticipation of Frashokereti infuses Zoroastrian teachings with a sense of hope and cosmic optimism. It emphasizes that, despite the struggles between light and darkness, the divine plan is one of ultimate reconciliation and unity. The temporary suffering of souls in the House of Lies is seen as a necessary process, allowing the universe to reach a state of equilibrium where all beings are once again aligned with asha. This belief not only shapes the Zoroastrian understanding of life after death but also guides practitioners in their daily lives, reminding them of the importance of striving for truth and purity, knowing that every action contributes to the greater cosmic balance.

Throughout these teachings, there is a deep respect for the role of free will. Zoroastrianism acknowledges that each individual has the freedom to choose their path, to align themselves with either the forces of light or the shadows of druj. This freedom is seen as both a gift and a responsibility, as it empowers each soul to shape its destiny. The journey of the soul through life and into the afterlife is a reflection of these choices, where the consequences are not merely imposed by a distant deity but are the natural outcomes of the soul's alignment—or misalignment—with the divine order.

For practitioners, this vision of the afterlife serves as a constant reminder of the impact of their choices. The knowledge that each thought, word, and deed contributes to the soul's journey across the Chinvat Bridge encourages a life of mindfulness and dedication to asha. It is a call to live with integrity, to cultivate light within oneself, and to extend that light through acts of kindness, honesty, and service. In this way, the Zoroastrian path is not one of fear but of aspiration—an invitation to walk the bridge with grace, guided by the eternal presence of Ahura Mazda.

This understanding of life after death also shapes the way Zoroastrians honor their departed. Rituals for the deceased focus on aiding the soul's journey, offering prayers and recitations that call upon Ahura Mazda to guide and protect the spirit during its transition. The tradition of lighting a fire or candle during these rites symbolizes the hope that the soul will find its way through the darkness and into the realm of light. These practices are not only acts of remembrance but also a way of maintaining a spiritual connection with the departed, reinforcing the belief that the bonds between souls endure beyond physical existence.

The journey of the soul, as depicted in Zoroastrianism, is thus a journey of continuous striving—striving to live in harmony with the divine, striving to overcome the temptations of darkness, and ultimately, striving to reach the realm where light and truth prevail. It is a path that does not end with death but continues beyond, where the echoes of each life resonate through the halls of the spiritual realm, contributing to the grand symphony of creation. And in this understanding, death is not a finality but a passage, a doorway through which the soul steps, carrying the light it has kindled within itself into a new and eternal dawn.

The transition of the soul beyond the physical world is an intricate journey, and for practitioners of Zoroastrianism, assisting their departed loved ones is a sacred duty. Through ancient rituals and prayers, the living can provide guidance and support to those who have crossed the threshold into the spiritual realm.

One of the central practices is the recitation of specific prayers and mantras, designed to aid the soul during its passage across the Chinvat Bridge. Among these, the Ashem Vohu and the Yatha Ahu Vairyo hold particular significance. These prayers, embodying the essence of asha (truth) and the divine order, are believed to offer spiritual strength to the soul, helping it to align with the cosmic principles that guide the journey towards the House of Song. For the Zoroastrian faithful, the repetition of these sacred verses is a way to invoke the presence of Ahura Mazda, creating a bridge of light that spans the realms of the living and the dead.

To perform these rites effectively, a quiet and sacred space is essential—one where the connection with the spiritual realm can be most deeply felt. Zoroastrians often light a candle or a small flame during these prayers, a symbolic gesture representing the Light Divine that guides the departed through the darkness. The flame is seen as a beacon, offering warmth and direction, ensuring that the soul remains oriented towards the path of asha. As the candle burns, the prayers flow, each word carrying the hope that the soul will find peace and clarity in its new existence.

The Fravahar, a symbol often depicted as a winged figure, also plays a crucial role in rituals for the departed. This ancient emblem represents the guardian spirit that remains with an individual throughout life and continues to guide them even in the afterlife. By invoking the Fravahar in ceremonies, practitioners seek to strengthen the protective energies around the soul, offering it guidance as it navigates the challenges of the afterlife. The invocation of the Fravahar reminds the living of the ongoing journey of the soul and the eternal nature of the spiritual bond that transcends death.

Another essential ritual is the remembrance ceremony, often performed on key dates such as the fourth, tenth, and thirtieth day after death. These milestones are considered significant as the soul is believed to undergo various stages of transformation during this time. On each of these days, families gather to offer prayers and to share stories of the deceased, reflecting on the virtues they embodied and the light they brought into the world. This act of communal memory serves not only to comfort the grieving but also to honor the soul's contributions to asha, reinforcing its connection to the Light Divine. The shared remembrance becomes a collective prayer, a chorus that reaches out across the realms.

In addition to prayers and rituals, Zoroastrianism encourages acts of charity and kindness in memory of the departed. These acts are seen as extensions of the deceased's own spirit, helping to cleanse any remaining attachments they may have to the material world. By engaging in charitable deeds—such as offering food to those in need, supporting community projects, or contributing to the upkeep of fire temples—practitioners believe that they assist the departed soul in its spiritual ascent. These acts of service are viewed as a continuation of the individual's journey toward light, enabling the soul to shed residual shadows and embrace its higher nature.

The practice of dakhma or the Tower of Silence, while less common today, represents another significant aspect of Zoroastrian death rituals. This ancient custom, where the deceased are exposed to the elements to prevent the pollution of the earth, reflects the deep respect for nature that permeates Zoroastrian beliefs. Although modern adaptations may replace this practice, the underlying principle remains: the importance of maintaining purity and respecting the cycles of life and death. The air, the sun, and the earth play a part in returning the physical form to the natural order, while the soul continues its journey to the realms beyond. This reverence for the natural world is a reminder of the interconnectedness of all life, a theme that resonates deeply throughout Zoroastrian teachings.

The memory of ancestors, too, holds a sacred place in Zoroastrian homes. Many families maintain small altars or sacred spaces dedicated to their forebears, where offerings of flowers, food, and water are made. These gestures, simple yet profound, are believed to nourish the spirits of those who have passed, maintaining a flow of love and gratitude between the living and the deceased. In such moments, the presence of the ancestors is not a distant memory but a living reality, woven into the fabric of daily life and prayer. Through these rituals, the boundaries between worlds become permeable, allowing the light of remembrance to shine through.

For those seeking a more profound spiritual connection, meditations focused on the departed can also be a powerful practice. By entering a state of deep calm, practitioners can focus their thoughts on the soul of the departed, visualizing them surrounded by a gentle, guiding light. This light, emanating from Ahura Mazda, is imagined to envelop the soul, offering it peace and direction. As the meditation deepens, the practitioner may sense a subtle communication, a quiet exchange between the realms that brings comfort and clarity to both the living and the departed. This practice serves as a reminder that even in death, the soul's journey is a continuation, and that the bonds of love can guide it through the mysteries of the afterlife.

Through these practices and ceremonies, Zoroastrianism offers a way to navigate the profound mystery of death. It is not viewed as an end but as a transformation, a passage from the physical to the spiritual, where the soul's journey takes on new dimensions. The rituals for the departed provide solace, not just for the living who mourn, but for the soul itself, ensuring that it is supported and guided as it enters the next phase of its existence. In these rites, one can perceive the echoes of a much larger cosmic rhythm—one where every soul, through the trials and triumphs of its life, contributes to the unfolding of a divine order.

Zoroastrian rituals for the deceased also reflect the broader philosophy of hope and redemption that permeates the faith. Even those souls who struggle through the shadows of the afterlife are believed to eventually find their way to the light. The prayers and offerings made by the living are part of this process, small beacons that illuminate the path toward Frashokereti, the ultimate renewal where all are restored to the divine light. It is a faith in the eventual triumph of good, in the healing power of love, and in the eternal embrace of Ahura Mazda that awaits every soul.

For those left behind, the practice of these rituals becomes an act of love and a reaffirmation of the divine principles that Zoroastrianism holds dear. It reminds them that their role in the cosmic order extends beyond life's earthly concerns, touching the very fabric of the universe. By honoring the departed, by guiding them with prayers and light, the living partake in a sacred dance—a dance where life, death, and rebirth are but movements in the grand symphony orchestrated by Ahura Mazda. And in this dance, there is a promise that no soul is ever truly lost, that each step, each prayer, brings it closer to the Light Divine that binds all creation.

Chapter 20
Spiritual Healing Techniques

In the rich tradition of Zoroastrianism, the path to spiritual healing is as ancient as it is profound. It weaves together the energies of the natural world, sacred elements, and divine invocations, offering a holistic approach to restoring balance and harmony within the self. Spiritual healing in this context is not merely a remedy for physical ailments but an intricate process that purifies the mind, body, and spirit, aligning the individual with the Light Divine.

Central to the practice of spiritual healing in Zoroastrianism is the use of the sacred fire. The fire, known as Atar, is considered the living embodiment of purity, a direct channel to Ahura Mazda's divine energy. In the context of healing, the presence of a burning flame serves as a beacon of light and warmth, helping to dispel spiritual impurities. A simple yet powerful ritual involves sitting before a fire, focusing on its steady glow, and reciting the Ashem Vohu. This prayer, imbued with the essence of asha (truth), harmonizes the vibrations of the environment and helps to cleanse the practitioner's aura of negative influences.

The practitioner can further enhance this ritual by placing specific herbs into the fire. Traditionally, Zoroastrians have used sandalwood, frankincense, and haoma, an ancient plant believed to hold sacred properties. The smoke that rises from these burning offerings is thought to carry prayers to the divine, creating a bridge between the earthly and spiritual realms. As the incense spirals upward, it also purifies the air around the practitioner, filling the space with a soothing presence that facilitates healing.

The act of breathing in this fragrant smoke while focusing on the divine is believed to restore the flow of energy within the body, allowing for a deeper connection with the Light Divine.

Another potent method of spiritual healing in Zoroastrianism involves the use of ab-zor—pure water blessed with prayers. Water, like fire, holds a sacred status in Zoroastrian belief, symbolizing both physical and spiritual purity. During a purification ritual, practitioners recite sacred verses over a vessel of water, asking Ahura Mazda to infuse it with divine healing energy. This blessed water can then be used for washing the face and hands or sprinkled throughout the home to cleanse negative energies. The act of anointing oneself with this water, particularly on the forehead and heart, is believed to open the spiritual centers of the body, promoting clarity of mind and a sense of inner peace.

The process of breathing exercises also plays a significant role in Zoroastrian healing practices. Through mindful breathing, one learns to synchronize their breath with the rhythm of the universe, drawing in the energies of the Light Divine and releasing impurities with each exhalation. A common technique is to breathe deeply while visualizing a golden light entering through the crown of the head, descending through the body, and enveloping the heart. As the practitioner exhales, they imagine this light expanding outward, dissolving any shadows or negativity. This method serves not only to calm the mind but also to revitalize the spirit, allowing for a more profound experience of connectedness with the cosmic order.

Recitation of mantras also forms a cornerstone of the Zoroastrian approach to spiritual healing. The Yatha Ahu Vairyo, for example, is a mantra that calls upon the power of Ahura Mazda to bring balance and healing. Repeating this mantra creates a resonance that purifies the practitioner's energy field, aligning their intentions with the will of the divine. The vibrations of the words, when spoken with focus and devotion, are believed to cleanse the subtle layers of the soul, facilitating a return to inner equilibrium. Practitioners often combine the chanting of mantras with the presence of fire or blessed water, creating a multi-layered approach to healing that addresses the body, mind, and spirit simultaneously.

Herbal remedies also find their place within Zoroastrian healing traditions. Haoma, both as a plant and a spiritual symbol, is of particular importance. In ancient times, haoma was prepared as a sacred drink during rituals, believed to possess life-giving properties. While the exact plant identified as haoma may have varied over time, its symbolic role as a healer and purifier remains central. Today, practitioners may use related herbs, such as asafetida or esfand (wild rue), which are burned to cleanse spaces and ward off harmful energies. The scent of these herbs, when released through the heat of fire, is thought to carry away impurities, leaving behind a purified atmosphere that promotes spiritual well-being.

Moreover, the ritual of Kushti, the tying and untying of the sacred cord worn by Zoroastrians, is an integral part of daily purification and spiritual protection. The Kushti is not merely a garment but a physical manifestation of the practitioner's commitment to the path of asha. Each time it is wrapped around the body, it is accompanied by recitations of prayers that reaffirm the individual's dedication to the Light Divine. When performed with intent, this daily ritual becomes a moment of recalibration, a time to realign one's thoughts and actions with the cosmic order. It serves as a reminder that the healing journey is ongoing, a daily act of maintaining harmony with the universe.

A deeper practice involves the use of guided meditations to connect with the Amesha Spentas, the divine entities that represent different aspects of Ahura Mazda's creation. For example, meditating on Haurvatat, the Amesha Spenta associated with wholeness and well-being, can help to invoke feelings of completeness and vitality. During this meditation, the practitioner visualizes a serene lake, representing Haurvatat's essence, and imagines immersing themselves in its healing waters. This visualization technique not only promotes a sense of inner tranquility but also serves as a spiritual invitation for the energies of Haurvatat to support the practitioner's healing process.

Music, too, has its place within the Zoroastrian approach to healing. The chanting of gathas—hymns attributed to Zoroaster—creates a sacred soundscape that vibrates with the principles of truth and light. When sung or listened to with focused attention, these ancient hymns are believed to harmonize the mind and heart, allowing for the release of emotional blockages. The resonance of the sacred sounds can help the listener feel more attuned to the divine rhythms of the universe, fostering a deeper sense of peace and clarity. Many practitioners find solace in these melodies, using them as tools for self-reflection and healing.

As these techniques demonstrate, the path to spiritual healing in Zoroastrianism is not linear but multi-faceted, involving the engagement of the senses, the focus of the mind, and the devotion of the heart. Whether through fire, water, breath, or sacred words, each practice serves to draw the practitioner closer to the essence of Ahura Mazda, allowing the divine light to penetrate and heal the shadows within. The rituals and practices described here are not just ancient traditions; they are living pathways, guiding those who seek them toward a deeper understanding of their own spiritual nature and the divine forces that shape the cosmos. Through these sacred practices, the seeker learns to become a vessel for the Light Divine, channeling its healing energies into every aspect of their life and being.

Central to these advanced healing methods is the precise preparation of herbal infusions and sacred incenses, which play a crucial role in Zoroastrian rituals. Herbs like esfand (wild rue) and sandalwood are not only symbols of purification but are also believed to possess inherent energies that can aid in spiritual cleansing. To create a healing atmosphere, practitioners can prepare a blend of dried esfand and sandalwood, burning it slowly on a charcoal disc placed in a fireproof vessel. As the smoke rises, it is essential to recite prayers such as the Ashem Vohu or the Yatha Ahu Vairyo, guiding the intention of the ritual toward the expulsion of negative influences. The practitioner allows the fragrant smoke to fill the space, visualizing it as a cloud of protective light that envelops both the physical environment and their own aura, dispelling any lingering spiritual impurities.

This practice can be enhanced by incorporating specific invocations to the Amesha Spentas, the divine entities that govern aspects of spiritual well-being. For example, calling upon Spenta Armaiti, the spirit of devotion and harmony with the earth, can be particularly effective when seeking to ground oneself and restore inner calm. To do this, practitioners place a small bowl of blessed water beside the burning incense, dedicating it to Spenta Armaiti and asking for her assistance in bringing peace and healing to their surroundings. As the water absorbs the prayers and the smoke mingles with the air, the ritual space becomes a conduit for divine energy, fostering a deeper connection with the cosmic forces of healing.

In addition to these rituals, guided meditations focusing on the elements—fire, water, earth, and air—offer a potent method for aligning the body's energy centers with the universal flow of asha. A meditation on fire, for instance, involves sitting in a darkened room with a single candle or a small flame, using its steady light as a focal point. The practitioner breathes deeply, visualizing the fire's warmth penetrating their chest, spreading outwards to each limb and filling them with a vibrant, golden light. This visualization helps to dissolve emotional blockages and fill the body with a renewed sense of vitality, as if the flames themselves are burning away any heaviness or shadows that have accumulated within the spirit.

Similarly, water meditations can be performed by sitting near a flowing stream or even in the quietude of one's home with a bowl of pure water. By placing their hands over the water and reciting sacred verses, practitioners can imbue the liquid with the energies of healing, using it to anoint their forehead, heart, and hands. This act symbolizes the washing away of inner burdens and the renewal of the spirit. The sound of flowing water, whether natural or recorded, can further deepen the meditative state, allowing the practitioner to feel as though they are merging with the rhythms of nature itself, guided by Haurvatat, the guardian of wholeness.

Beyond the elements, advanced healing also involves the crafting of sacred talismans or afrinagans, objects imbued with prayers that serve as focal points for divine energy. Practitioners can create these by inscribing Zoroastrian symbols or sacred names onto small pieces of parchment or stone, then blessing these inscriptions with invocations to Ahura Mazda and the Amesha Spentas. These talismans are carried as personal items of protection or placed in the home as guardians against negative forces. The process of creating an afrinagan is a ritual in itself, requiring focus and spiritual purity, as the practitioner meditates on the protective power they wish to channel into the object. The talisman then serves as a physical anchor, reminding them of their continuous connection to the Light Divine and the protective energies of the spiritual realm.

For those seeking to heal others, Zoroastrian spiritual healing also includes ritualistic laying on of hands, a method that transfers the energy of the Light Divine directly from the practitioner to the recipient. This practice involves placing one's hands gently on or near the affected area of the person needing healing while reciting mantras such as the Yatha Ahu Vairyo. The practitioner visualizes a stream of golden light flowing from their hands, permeating the recipient's body and filling it with warmth and divine energy. This method is not about the practitioner's personal power but rather about acting as a conduit through which the divine energies of Ahura Mazda flow, bringing restoration to the person in need.

It is crucial, however, for practitioners to prepare themselves spiritually before attempting to heal others. This preparation involves performing purification rituals on themselves, such as washing hands and face with blessed water, and offering prayers for guidance and protection. The integrity and purity of the healer's own spirit are essential in ensuring that the energies being transferred remain untainted and beneficial. The healer's mindset should be one of humility and dedication to the well-being of others, seeing themselves as a vessel for the divine grace that flows through all things.

Another powerful aspect of advanced healing practices is the recitation of extended prayers and gathas during the dawn or dusk, times when the veil between the physical and spiritual worlds is believed to be thinner. The Gathas, the hymns composed by Zoroaster, are filled with deep spiritual insights and have a vibration that resonates with the cosmic order. By reciting these ancient words with reverence, practitioners align themselves with the original intentions of the Prophet, allowing the timeless wisdom of the Gathas to permeate their consciousness. This practice serves to reattune the practitioner's energy field, strengthening their spiritual resilience and creating an atmosphere where healing can naturally occur.

Creating a space dedicated to these rituals is also recommended for those pursuing deeper spiritual healing. A small altar with representations of the sacred elements—such as a candle for fire, a bowl of water, a small dish of earth, and a feather for air—can become a focal point for meditation and prayer. This altar serves as a reminder of the practitioner's connection to the divine and the natural world, providing a place of refuge for reflection and renewal. During healing sessions, the practitioner can offer small tokens, like flowers or grains, to the altar, as acts of gratitude to Ahura Mazda and the cosmic forces that guide the healing process.

In the realm of dreams, Zoroastrianism recognizes the potential for profound spiritual healing. Practitioners are encouraged to seek guidance through dreams, using rituals before sleep to invite messages from Ahura Mazda and the Amesha Spentas. Lighting a small lamp beside the bed and offering a prayer for clarity can open the channels of communication between the conscious mind and the spiritual world. Upon waking, it is important to record any dreams that feel significant, as these can hold symbols or insights that aid in the healing journey. Reflecting on these dream messages can provide a deeper understanding of the internal conflicts or emotional wounds that require attention.

Chapter 21
The Divine Nature of the Human Being

Zoroastrianism holds a profound belief in the divine potential of every human being, viewing each individual as a unique expression of Ahura Mazda's will. At the heart of this belief lies the concept that every person has a fragment of the divine light within, a spark that connects them directly to the cosmic order and the path of asha. Unlike some traditions that see humanity as fundamentally flawed, Zoroastrian teachings emphasize the capacity for goodness, wisdom, and spiritual growth inherent in all.

Central to Zoroastrian anthropology is the concept of fravashi, often understood as a guardian spirit or higher self that exists beyond the limitations of the physical body. The fravashi is both a guide and a reflection of the divine essence that exists within each soul. It serves as a reminder of the sacred origin of the individual, a celestial blueprint that encourages humans to strive for their highest potential. Zoroastrians believe that the fravashi accompanies a person from birth, guiding them towards the fulfillment of their spiritual duties and aiding in their struggle against the forces of druj—the cosmic lies and distortions that lead one away from the path of truth.

The recognition of the fravashi is not only a reminder of divine origin but also a call to responsibility. It implies that every individual has an active role in shaping the world according to the principles of asha. Through conscious actions, humans participate in the cosmic battle between asha (truth) and druj (falsehood), with their thoughts, words, and deeds tipping the scales. This belief in the active role of human choice is central to the

Zoroastrian understanding of free will. It suggests that while each person carries within them the potential for divine alignment, it is their choices that determine whether they contribute to the light or fall into the shadows of ignorance and destruction.

The idea of free will, or khyvana, is intertwined with moral and spiritual growth. It is seen as a gift from Ahura Mazda, allowing humans to choose their alignment with the divine principles. This freedom is not without its challenges, as every decision carries the weight of ethical implications. Yet, it is through this freedom that the journey of the soul becomes meaningful. The struggle to choose rightly, amidst the temptations and distractions of the world, is what shapes the inner character of the practitioner, turning each moment into an opportunity for spiritual refinement.

Zoroastrian teachings suggest that the alignment with one's fravashi and the principles of asha brings about a state of spiritual clarity, where the individual becomes a conduit for the Light Divine. This alignment is not a static achievement but a dynamic process, where one continually engages with their inner divine nature through meditation, prayer, and self-reflection. Practitioners are encouraged to seek periods of solitude to listen to the whispers of their fravashi, often through simple yet profound practices such as reciting the Gathas—hymns believed to carry the words of Zoroaster himself. The rhythmic recitation of these ancient verses allows the mind to quiet, opening a space where the wisdom of the higher self can emerge, guiding the practitioner in their daily decisions.

The connection between humans and the divine also extends to the natural world, where Zoroastrianism sees a reflection of Ahura Mazda's creation in every element of nature. This perspective reinforces the belief that humans, as stewards of creation, carry a sacred duty to protect and honor the earth and its resources. The divine nature within humans calls them to act with reverence towards all life, seeing the world not as a resource to be exploited but as a living manifestation of the divine order. This belief shapes a Zoroastrian ethic of environmental care, where actions taken to preserve nature are seen as an extension of one's spiritual practice, aligning the individual more closely with the principles of asha.

In the teachings of Zoroaster, the divine spark within is also connected to the broader concept of the urvan, or soul, which embodies the essence of an individual's consciousness. The urvan is the traveler on the spiritual journey, guided by the fravashi and constantly shaped by the choices made through free will. At the time of death, the urvan is believed to cross the Chinvat Bridge, where it is judged based on its adherence to truth and justice. This judgment is not merely a moment of reckoning but a reflection of the soul's alignment with its own divine nature throughout its earthly existence. A life lived in alignment with asha allows the urvan to ascend into the light, joining the divine presence of Ahura Mazda, while those who have strayed face the challenges of purification before they can return to the source.

Zoroastrian rituals often emphasize this journey of the soul, offering opportunities for practitioners to reconnect with their divine essence. Ceremonies like the Jashan, a communal celebration of gratitude, and personal acts of prayer and meditation are seen as ways to honor both the external divine order and the divine presence within. These rituals help to nurture the relationship between the urvan and the fravashi, creating a bridge between the material world and the spiritual truths that lie beyond it. Each prayer, each offering, each moment of silence becomes a reaffirmation of the divine potential that lies dormant within, waiting to be awakened through conscious intention.

The role of community is also significant in supporting individuals on this path. Zoroastrianism values the collective spiritual journey, where families and communities come together in the pursuit of truth and the celebration of the Light Divine. In shared rituals and gatherings, the divine spark within each person resonates with those around them, creating a powerful network of spiritual energy that strengthens the bonds between members and enhances their connection to Ahura Mazda. This sense of collective responsibility and mutual support helps to anchor individuals in their practice, providing the encouragement needed to continue on the path of spiritual evolution.

Recognizing the divine nature within oneself is not only about spiritual growth but also about embodying a higher standard of conduct in the world. Zoroastrian teachings call practitioners to be living examples of asha, allowing the Light Divine to shine through their actions. This is reflected in the emphasis on Spenta Mainyu, the beneficent spirit that guides the pursuit of good thoughts, good words, and good deeds. To live in accordance with Spenta Mainyu is to recognize that the divine within is not separate from the divine around; it is a call to manifest that light in every interaction, every decision, and every moment of life.

The divine nature of the human being, as taught in Zoroastrianism, thus becomes a compass guiding the soul through the complexities of existence. It challenges individuals to see beyond the surface of their daily lives, to recognize the sacredness in each breath, and to realize that within their very essence lies the capacity for transformation.

The path to recognizing one's divine nature begins with the practice of khshnūman, a form of prayer and meditation that focuses on harmonizing the mind with the higher self. Practitioners are encouraged to find a quiet space, ideally near a source of light such as a candle or a fire, symbolizing the presence of Ahura Mazda. With each breath, they visualize the light entering their body, filling them from within, and radiating outward. This simple yet profound practice is meant to remind the individual of the light that resides within them, a direct reflection of the divine spark that connects them to the eternal.

In the quiet of this meditation, thoughts and distractions often arise, but Zoroastrian practice views these as opportunities to exercise the discipline of khshathra, or self-control. As the mind wanders, the practitioner gently brings their focus back to the light, learning to observe their thoughts without attachment. This act of gentle redirection symbolizes the larger spiritual journey, where the distractions of druj—falsehood and illusion—

are acknowledged but not allowed to dominate. Over time, this practice cultivates a sense of inner clarity, allowing the urvan (soul) to feel the presence of the fravashi more clearly, guiding their actions and thoughts.

Another essential practice in aligning with one's divine nature is dahma, or the cultivation of good thoughts. This involves a conscious effort to replace negative or destructive thoughts with those that align with the principles of asha. Throughout the day, practitioners are encouraged to pause and reflect on their thoughts, asking themselves whether these thoughts bring them closer to the light or deepen the shadows within. This reflective practice is not about repressing negative emotions but transforming them into opportunities for growth. For example, anger can be transmuted into a desire for justice, and fear into a deeper trust in Ahura Mazda's guidance.

Zoroastrianism also emphasizes the power of manthra, sacred words that carry the vibration of divine wisdom. Regular recitation of these mantras, such as Ashem Vohu (the mantra of truth and righteousness) and Yatha Ahu Vairyo (the mantra of divine choice), becomes a tool for aligning the mind with higher principles. Each mantra is more than a spoken word; it is a vibration that resonates with the divine light within, helping to cleanse the mind of impurities and attune it to the cosmic order. Practitioners are encouraged to integrate these recitations into their morning and evening routines, using them as moments of recalibration, where the voice of the fravashi can be heard more clearly.

An important aspect of embracing one's divine nature involves confronting the shadows within—the fears, doubts, and past actions that may cloud the light. The process of paiti, or repentance, is a sacred act in Zoroastrianism that allows individuals to reflect on their mistakes and seek alignment with asha. This is not a practice of self-recrimination but one of honest self-assessment, where the individual acknowledges where they have strayed and makes a conscious commitment to realign with their higher self. Rituals of purification, such as washing the hands and face with water while reciting prayers, help to symbolize this inner cleansing, offering a fresh start each day.

To further deepen the connection with the divine, the practice of gratitude (spas) becomes a daily ritual. Zoroastrianism teaches that expressing gratitude is a way to recognize the presence of the divine in every aspect of life. By consciously giving thanks for the simple blessings—a meal, the warmth of the sun, the presence of loved ones—practitioners begin to see the fingerprints of Ahura Mazda in all things. This shift in perspective allows the individual to live in a state of reverence, where every moment becomes an opportunity to acknowledge the light that permeates all of existence.

Practical exercises such as journaling also serve as a means for deeper self-discovery. Practitioners are encouraged to keep a journal of their thoughts, dreams, and reflections on the day's events, noting moments when they felt in alignment with their divine nature and times when they struggled. This practice of reflection, done regularly, allows the individual to see patterns and learn from their experiences, using them as a guide for future actions. It serves as a written dialogue with one's fravashi, where the challenges and triumphs of the spiritual journey are recorded and used for deeper introspection.

Another way to honor the divine essence within is through acts of arash, or selfless service. By helping others without seeking personal gain, the practitioner embodies the principles of Spenta Mainyu, the spirit of benevolence and creativity. Such acts are not only seen as a moral duty but as a way to purify the soul, for they reflect the giving nature of Ahura Mazda. Simple actions—offering a meal to the hungry, caring for animals, or participating in community rituals—become expressions of the divine light, nurturing the connection between the individual and the greater cosmic order.

The relationship between the inner divine and the natural world is also nurtured through practices that connect the practitioner with the elements. Zoroastrian rituals often include offerings to the earth, fire, and water as a way to recognize the sacredness of these elements and their role in sustaining life. Spending time in nature, whether in meditation by a flowing river or walking through a forest, helps to ground the practitioner in the rhythms of creation, reminding them of their place within the greater tapestry of life. This practice of frith, or sacred connection with nature, serves as a reminder that the divine is not confined to temples or prayers but is present in the very fabric of the world around them.

Embracing the divine nature within oneself also means embracing the path of continuous learning. Zoroastrianism values wisdom as a means to deepen one's understanding of the universe and the divine. Practitioners are encouraged to study the Gathas and other sacred texts, not merely as historical documents but as living guides for their own spiritual journey. Through reading, discussion, and contemplation, the teachings of Zoroaster come alive, offering new insights into the mysteries of existence and the workings of the divine mind.

Community gatherings, such as the gahanbar festivals, provide opportunities for shared learning and spiritual renewal. In these gatherings, stories of Zoroaster and the yasna (rituals of worship) are retold, serving as a means to reinforce the shared values and spiritual goals of the community. In these communal spaces, the individual feels the strength of the collective divine light, which supports and uplifts their personal journey. The presence of others who are walking the same path serves as a mirror, reflecting the potential for growth and reminding each practitioner that they are not alone in their quest for divine connection.

Through consistent practice, the divine spark within begins to illuminate not only the inner life of the practitioner but also their actions in the world. They become a living testament to the teachings of Zoroaster, embodying asha in their thoughts, words, and deeds. And as their connection to their inner fravashi strengthens, they find themselves more attuned to the whispers of the divine, guiding them towards a life of greater wisdom, compassion, and spiritual clarity. The journey towards realizing the divine nature within is thus both a return to one's origins and a forward movement into the ever-unfolding mystery of the Light Divine.

Chapter 22
The Covenant with Ahura Mazda

In the Zoroastrian tradition, Ahura Mazda, the Wise Lord, is not a distant deity but a presence that seeks a personal relationship with every soul. This connection is symbolized in the daily prayers and rituals that bring the practitioner closer to the divine essence. These practices act as reminders of the spiritual responsibilities that come with this covenant—promoting truth, protecting creation, and nurturing the inner light that reflects Ahura Mazda's wisdom.

One of the most significant aspects of this covenant is the Yazna, a sacred commitment where the individual dedicates themselves to the principles of asha. This commitment is renewed daily through the recitation of prayers like Ashem Vohu, which emphasizes the value of righteousness, and Yatha Ahu Vairyo, which celebrates the divine order. In these prayers, the practitioner declares their allegiance to the path of light, pledging to embody the qualities of wisdom, kindness, and truth in their thoughts, words, and deeds.

The Kushti ritual, where a sacred thread is tied around the waist, is another physical manifestation of this covenant. Each time the thread is tied, it serves as a reminder of the vows made to Ahura Mazda, a symbol of the practitioner's commitment to purity and truth. The daily act of untying and retying the Kushti thread is a reaffirmation of the devotee's dedication to live according to the divine will, turning ordinary moments into opportunities for spiritual renewal.

The nature of the covenant extends beyond individual devotion. It is a call to actively participate in the cosmic struggle between light and darkness, aligning oneself with the creative and positive forces of Spenta Mainyu. This alignment is expressed in the practice of Khvarenah, the divine glory that each soul can cultivate by following the path of asha. By consciously choosing to act with righteousness, the practitioner becomes a vessel through which the divine light can manifest in the world, contributing to the ongoing creation and maintenance of order against the forces of chaos.

Yet, the covenant with Ahura Mazda is not one of blind obedience. It invites questioning, understanding, and growth. Zoroastrian teachings encourage the use of Vohu Manah—the Good Mind—to engage with the divine will thoughtfully. Practitioners are urged to seek wisdom, to reflect deeply on the nature of their choices, and to strive for a balance between free will and alignment with divine wisdom. This dynamic relationship allows the practitioner to grow spiritually, using their understanding to navigate the complexities of life while remaining faithful to the principles of asha.

The teachings of Zaratustra emphasize that this sacred bond is not just a matter of individual spirituality but has broader implications for the community and the world. A person who honors their covenant with Ahura Mazda is expected to act as a guardian of creation, respecting all forms of life and contributing to the well-being of the world. This responsibility extends to protecting the environment, treating others with fairness, and working for the greater good. It is a reminder that every action, no matter how small, contributes to the larger cosmic struggle between light and darkness.

Within this covenant, the practice of paiti, or self-reflection, becomes a vital tool for spiritual progress. Practitioners regularly engage in introspection, asking themselves whether their actions are in harmony with the divine will and the path of asha. This process of self-assessment is not about harsh judgment but about realignment, ensuring that one's thoughts, words, and actions remain true to the principles that they have pledged to uphold. Through this practice, the bond with Ahura Mazda becomes a living reality, guiding the practitioner through both challenges and moments of joy.

The covenant with Ahura Mazda also highlights the importance of humility. Recognizing the divine wisdom that transcends human understanding, practitioners approach their spiritual path with a sense of reverence and awe. This humility does not negate the value of human agency but acknowledges the vastness of the divine plan in which each individual plays a part. It is this humility that opens the practitioner's heart to the guidance of the fravashi, the inner divine spark, allowing them to navigate the complexities of life with grace.

In the daily expressions of gratitude (spas), practitioners honor the blessings they receive from Ahura Mazda, recognizing that each gift—whether it be life, knowledge, or the presence of loved ones—is part of the divine flow. Through these expressions of thankfulness, the practitioner keeps the covenant alive in their heart, turning every moment into a chance to acknowledge the presence of the divine. This gratitude deepens the bond, creating a cycle of giving and receiving where the human soul and divine spirit are intertwined.

Moreover, the sacred festivals, like Nowruz and the Gahanbar celebrations, serve as communal renewals of this covenant. During these times, the community comes together to honor the divine, to celebrate the cycles of nature, and to express their collective commitment to the principles of Zoroastrianism. These festivals are not only times of joy but are deeply spiritual events where the bond between humanity and the divine is reaffirmed, and the community rededicates itself to the path of light.

This covenant is not a static contract but a living relationship that evolves with the practitioner's understanding and growth. As the individual deepens their spiritual practice, the covenant becomes a source of strength and guidance, a compass that points towards the divine in every aspect of life. It is a relationship built on mutual respect, where Ahura Mazda's wisdom flows through the practitioner's life, guiding their steps towards greater understanding and fulfillment.

Ultimately, the covenant with Ahura Mazda is a path of transformation. It calls the practitioner to rise above the mundane concerns of the world, to see life through the lens of the divine, and to act in ways that reflect the light of asha. This transformation is not always easy, for it requires the practitioner to confront their own shadows and strive towards a higher standard of being. Yet, in this struggle, they find the essence of their spiritual journey—a journey that brings them closer to the divine and to their true self.

By embracing this sacred bond, the practitioner becomes a co-creator in the ongoing story of light and creation. They become a living testament to the power of choice and the potential of the human spirit to reflect the divine light. And in every prayer, every act of kindness, and every moment of reflection, they renew their commitment to the covenant, finding within it the source of strength that guides them through the ever-unfolding mystery of the divine.

To deepen one's relationship with Ahura Mazda and the sacred covenant that underpins Zoroastrian practice, rituals of renewal serve as pivotal moments. These rituals reinforce the bond between the practitioner and the divine, allowing a continuous flow of spiritual energy and purpose.

One of the most essential rituals of renewal is the Navjote ceremony, which marks the initiation of an individual into the Zoroastrian faith. While this ceremony is typically a once-in-a-lifetime event for young initiates, its essence can be mirrored in periodic personal rituals where the practitioner reaffirms their vows to Ahura Mazda. This renewal can be as simple as taking a moment of solitude, lighting a fire or candle, and reciting core prayers like the Yatha Ahu Vairyo and Ashem Vohu, while reflecting on the commitment to uphold truth and righteousness. Through these actions, the practitioner revitalizes the spiritual energies that connect them to the divine.

Creating a sacred space is fundamental for these rituals of renewal. Whether in a dedicated room, a quiet corner, or an altar adorned with a small flame, a clear space helps to focus the mind and spirit. Cleanse this space with the elements—sprinkling water, fanning smoke from a purifying incense, or simply ensuring a clean and orderly environment. This preparation is not just physical but spiritual, aligning the space with the purity that Ahura Mazda represents. As the practitioner prepares this space, they prepare their own heart and mind for the deeper connection that the ritual fosters.

The recitation of the Fravahar prayer, dedicated to the guiding spiritual essence within, is another profound practice. This prayer helps to awaken the connection with the fravashi, the higher self that remains in tune with the divine. By focusing on the words and their meaning, the practitioner connects more deeply with the divine purpose and their role in the unfolding of cosmic order. This practice of invoking the fravashi is particularly potent during moments of doubt or spiritual weariness, as it serves to remind the practitioner of their inner light and the support of the divine.

Another powerful method of renewing the covenant with Ahura Mazda is through the practice of Baj. This involves a state of concentrated, silent prayer where the mind is fully attuned to the divine. The Baj can be performed before significant moments or tasks, serving as a way to invoke divine guidance and protection. For practitioners seeking to renew their spiritual focus, dedicating a session of Baj with specific intentions—such as the desire for wisdom, the strength to overcome challenges, or the will to remain steadfast in the path of asha—can be transformative. It is a ritual that aligns the thoughts directly with the divine frequency, making each action that follows an extension of one's spiritual will.

Rituals of renewal also encompass community gatherings, such as Gahambar festivals, where practitioners come together to honor the creation and the ongoing relationship with Ahura Mazda. Even though these are communal events, individuals can draw upon their energy for personal renewal. Participating in or organizing a small gathering of fellow practitioners, where hymns are sung, and prayers recited, can reignite the shared spiritual commitment that strengthens the bond with the divine. It is in these communal expressions that the covenant takes on a living form, manifesting not only in private devotion but in collective celebration.

For those who seek to deepen their covenant through daily routines, the simple yet profound act of gratitude plays a central role. Each day, before partaking in meals or before sleep, a moment can be taken to offer thanks to Ahura Mazda for the blessings received. A short prayer, such as Tandarosti—which means well-being and health—becomes a vehicle to align daily actions with the divine will. These expressions of gratitude serve to remind the practitioner that each aspect of life is interwoven with the divine presence and that their journey is part of a greater cosmic design.

Meditation on the divine light is another profound practice that helps renew the covenant. This can be done by visualizing a flame at the center of one's heart, symbolizing the eternal light of Ahura Mazda. As the practitioner breathes slowly and deeply, they imagine this light expanding, filling their being and connecting them to the larger, universal light that guides all creation. This visualization serves not only as a form of meditation but as a direct experience of the divine presence, reminding the practitioner of their place within the cosmic order and their ongoing commitment to walk in the light.

The renewal of the covenant is also reinforced through the daily recital of Patet, the prayer of repentance. This practice is not about guilt but about consciously reflecting on any actions, thoughts, or words that may have deviated from the path of asha. By acknowledging these moments with humility, the practitioner opens themselves to the purifying energy of the divine and realigns with the principles of truth. It is an opportunity to let go of the past and step back into the light with a renewed spirit, stronger in their commitment to the divine path.

Another profound aspect of renewing the covenant is through direct service to others. Acts of charity, kindness, and community service are seen as expressions of one's devotion to Ahura Mazda. These actions are not separate from spiritual practice; they are its natural extension. In every act of service, the practitioner reaffirms their role as a steward of light, choosing to manifest divine virtues through tangible actions. Service becomes a prayer in motion, a living embodiment of the covenant that transforms the world around them.

Finally, there are special times in the Zoroastrian calendar, such as the monthly observance of Parab, where the practitioner is encouraged to focus on a specific spiritual theme. These observances can be used as opportunities for deeper self-reflection, fasting, or extended prayer sessions. During these times, the renewal of the covenant can be intensified through focused devotion, allowing the practitioner to realign their life with the cycles of nature and the divine rhythm that Ahura Mazda has woven into the cosmos.

In all these practices, the essence of renewing the covenant with Ahura Mazda lies in the conscious choice to remain in the flow of divine light. It is not merely a ritualistic repetition but a living relationship that deepens as the practitioner grows. Each act of devotion, each prayer whispered in solitude, and each kind deed performed is a thread that strengthens the bond with the divine. And in this continuous renewal, the practitioner finds a wellspring of spiritual strength, guiding them through the complexities of life and leading them ever closer to the radiant light of Ahura Mazda.

Chapter 23
Spiritual Renewal

The concept of spiritual renewal is a cornerstone of Zoroastrian practice, reflecting the belief that each soul has the potential to be reborn continuously through the embrace of divine light.

One of the most profound symbols of spiritual renewal in Zoroastrianism is the ritual of hamazor, the practice of unity and strength through connection. In this act, believers symbolically shake hands, transferring energy and blessings. While this practice is often done during festivals or communal gatherings, it carries a deeper significance for the individual. To perform a solitary version of hamazor, the practitioner can meditate on their hands' symbolic connection to the divine, visualizing the transfer of divine energy into their own being. This gesture serves as a reminder that spiritual renewal is not an isolated event but a reconnection with the greater energy flow that moves through the universe.

Another essential practice is the padyab, a ritual of ablution using pure water. Water, a symbol of life and cleansing, is used to purify the hands, face, and body before prayers or sacred rituals. But the deeper essence of the padyab lies in its metaphorical meaning—the washing away of spiritual impurities, of thoughts and actions that may have accumulated over time. It serves as a reminder that just as water cleanses the body, the act of self-reflection and repentance cleanses the spirit. The practitioner is encouraged to look inward during this process, identifying areas in life where they seek renewal and asking for Ahura Mazda's guidance to move beyond them.

The act of breathing, so often taken for granted, becomes a gateway to renewal when done with mindful intention. Zoroastrianism places great importance on the breath as a link between the physical and spiritual realms. By practicing Atash Niyayesh, the prayer to the fire, one can integrate breathwork with the focus on the inner flame. As the practitioner inhales, they visualize drawing in divine light, and as they exhale, they release any stagnant energies or negative thoughts. This practice serves as a mini-cycle of renewal with each breath, connecting the practitioner directly to the eternal flame that burns within and around them.

Renewal also finds expression through the Visperad, a high ritual that honors all aspects of creation and seeks to bring the practitioner back into harmony with the cosmos. While the complete Visperad is a ceremonial event led by priests, its essence can be incorporated into personal rituals of renewal. A simplified version involves setting an intention that aligns with a broader cosmic purpose—whether it be a wish for greater compassion, clarity, or resilience. As the practitioner recites prayers, they can envision this intention being carried forth into the universe, harmonizing their personal energies with those of Ahura Mazda's creation. This alignment with the divine will is a powerful act of spiritual rebirth, as it allows the practitioner to shed self-centered desires and embrace a vision of collective wellbeing.

The Zoroastrian calendar itself provides opportunities for spiritual renewal, with each of the Gahambars—seasonal festivals—inviting a deeper reflection on life's cycles. For example, during Maidyozarem, which celebrates the mid-spring harvest, practitioners focus on growth and renewal in their own lives. It becomes a time to plant new seeds, both physically in the earth and metaphorically in the soul. Through prayer and meditation, the practitioner considers what habits, thoughts, or behaviors they wish to cultivate or release, using the energy of the season to support their transformation. These seasonal reflections align the soul's inner journey with the outer rhythms of nature, making renewal a harmonious process with the world around.

Symbolic actions such as the lighting of candles or fires can also serve as a ritual of renewal. In a simple yet profound act, the practitioner lights a candle while reciting a verse from the Gathas—the hymns of Zoroaster. As the flame flickers to life, it represents the divine spark within each person, a reminder that, no matter how dimmed one's spirit may feel, there is always potential for rekindling. The flame becomes a visual metaphor for the soul's capacity to shine brightly, even amidst the challenges of existence. As the candle burns, the practitioner reflects on the aspects of their life they wish to illuminate, focusing on the inner shadows they seek to dispel.

Engaging with the natural elements is another path to spiritual renewal in Zoroastrianism. Practitioners are encouraged to spend time outdoors, feeling the wind on their face, the warmth of the sun, or the grounding energy of the earth beneath their feet. These moments become opportunities to draw upon the elemental energies that Ahura Mazda has infused into the world. Standing by a river or stream, one might meditate on the flow of the water as a symbol of life's continuous movement and the potential for renewal at every moment. These simple, mindful practices connect the practitioner to the eternal cycles of nature, offering a sense of renewal that is both spiritual and deeply embodied.

Zoroastrian teachings also emphasize the role of good deeds in the process of renewal. By actively choosing to perform Vohu Manah—acts of kindness and compassion—one contributes to the growth of their spiritual light. The practitioner is encouraged to think of each good deed as planting a seed in their spiritual garden. As these seeds grow, they produce fruits that nourish not only the soul but the world around them. Each act of kindness thus becomes a step toward personal transformation, renewing the soul's commitment to the path of asha and enhancing its connection with Ahura Mazda.

As a part of this continuous renewal, the practitioner may find themselves drawn to the practice of fasting and reflection during Zarathust-no-Diso, a day that honors the passing of Zoroaster. This period is not one of mourning but of introspection, a time to contemplate the teachings of Zoroaster and their application in one's life. Fasting, even if for a few hours, serves as a reminder of the body's dependence on spiritual nourishment, highlighting the importance of not only sustaining the physical self but also renewing the inner self. During this time, the practitioner might recite prayers, meditate on the life of Zoroaster, and reflect on how their own journey mirrors the search for truth and wisdom.

One powerful ritual for spiritual renewal involves the practice of Frashokereti, the idea of ultimate renewal and purification that extends to the entire cosmos. On a personal level, this concept can be internalized through a ritual bath that symbolizes the washing away of past burdens. The practitioner prepares a sacred space with a vessel of water, lighting candles or a small fire nearby to represent Ahura Mazda's eternal light. As they pour the water over their hands, they recite verses from the Avesta, envisioning the water carrying away negative energy, regrets, and emotional burdens. With each splash, a new sense of purity is imagined, allowing the spirit to emerge rejuvenated.

Alongside this ritual bath, the practice of Baj—prayers of consecration—serves as a method to realign oneself with the spiritual order. The Baj involves focusing on specific aspects of the divine and the cosmos while reciting precise prayers that invoke the blessings of the Amesha Spentas. During the ritual, the practitioner places their hands over the heart, a gesture that symbolizes the centering of divine energies within themselves. This practice can be particularly effective when paired with fasting or a period of quiet reflection, as it allows for deeper absorption of the spiritual insights and energies that accompany the prayer. Each recitation is a reminder that renewal is as much about listening to the divine as it is about active transformation.

Meditation is also central to the journey of spiritual renewal. For this, practitioners can engage in a meditation known as the "Light of the Dawn" visualization. This meditation is best performed at sunrise, aligning with the natural cycle of rebirth that each new day represents. The practitioner sits facing the east, where the sun rises, and closes their eyes, imagining a warm golden light entering through the crown of their head and filling their entire being. As they breathe slowly, this light is visualized flowing down the spine, spreading through the limbs, and illuminating even the deepest corners of the heart and mind. Each breath deepens the sense of connection to Ahura Mazda's light, allowing the practitioner to let go of shadows and receive clarity and insight.

To amplify the effects of this practice, one can incorporate the recitation of the Yasna Haptanghaiti, a hymn that praises the elements and honors the connection between the divine and the physical world. This hymn not only enhances the meditator's focus but also serves as a bridge to the energies of the earth, water, and sky—elements that carry the power of renewal in their cyclical movements. Reciting or listening to the Yasna creates a sacred space around the practitioner, weaving a cocoon of spiritual energy that supports their transformation.

Another profound way to experience spiritual renewal is through the ritual of releasing past grievances, known as the "Forgiveness Ceremony." This is a practice that emphasizes the Zoroastrian values of compassion and the purifying nature of forgiveness. The practitioner sits before a small fire or candle, symbolizing the divine witness, and writes down any regrets, grudges, or lingering resentments on pieces of paper. As each piece is read aloud, it is then burned in the flame, with a prayer to release these feelings and transform them into light. This act of burning is not merely symbolic; it represents the dissolution of old energies, allowing space for the new. The rising smoke is seen as carrying away these burdens, offering them to the divine for transformation.

This ceremony is particularly powerful during the Rapithwin season—a time when Zoroastrians celebrate the sun's strength and warmth. Aligning personal practices with this season reinforces the connection between the individual's inner journey and the rhythms of nature. The practitioner might choose to perform this ritual outdoors, feeling the sun's rays as they burn away the writings, merging the warmth of the outer sun with the inner fire of transformation. Through this process, the practitioner becomes more attuned to the asha, the cosmic order that guides all renewal.

Incorporating acts of gratitude into daily practice further deepens the sense of renewal. Each morning, upon rising, the practitioner is encouraged to recite the Khorshed Niyayesh—a prayer to the sun—that expresses gratitude for the light that sustains all life. Gratitude is seen as a vital component of spiritual renewal because it shifts the mind's focus from lack to abundance, from burdens to blessings. It serves as a reminder that even amidst challenges, the light of Ahura Mazda continues to shine, guiding the soul toward growth. Keeping a gratitude journal, noting small moments of beauty and kindness each day, becomes a simple yet potent way to remain attuned to this light.

For those seeking a more communal experience of renewal, participation in the Gahanbar festivals offers a collective ritual of rebirth. These seasonal celebrations are times of reflection and renewal, where Zoroastrians gather to honor creation and the cycles of life. The communal sharing of food, prayers, and reflections during these festivals creates a powerful energy of renewal that extends beyond the individual. It serves as a reminder that while each soul's journey is unique, renewal is a shared experience that binds the community together, just as each sunrise belongs to all who see it.

Personal retreats, even if for a single day, provide another avenue for deep renewal. A retreat can be as simple as setting aside a day for solitude, prayer, and reflection, away from the distractions of daily life. During this time, the practitioner engages in extended recitations of the Gathas and focuses on silence, allowing space for insights and inspirations to emerge. They might choose to fast or abstain from certain activities, focusing instead on what truly nourishes the soul. As the day progresses, the mind quiets, the spirit becomes more attuned to the rhythms of the heart, and the layers that obscure the inner light begin to dissolve.

An integral part of the renewal process involves embracing the shadows within oneself—the doubts, fears, and attachments that linger in the soul's depths. Zoroastrianism teaches that darkness can be transformed into light through conscious awareness. By sitting with these inner shadows during meditation, without judgment, the practitioner begins to understand their origins and how they can be released. This process mirrors the cosmic battle between light and darkness, yet within the microcosm of the self. As the practitioner integrates these aspects, they move closer to embodying the pure light of Ahura Mazda.

Chapter 24
The Power of Offerings

Offerings hold a special place in Zoroastrian practice, serving as acts of devotion and gratitude toward Ahura Mazda, the Creator. They are not merely gestures; they carry the essence of intention, symbolizing a tangible connection between the material world and the spiritual realms. In the ancient teachings, offerings are viewed as a way to express reverence, invite blessings, and maintain a harmonious relationship with the divine forces that govern the cosmos.

Central to the concept of offerings in Zoroastrianism is the idea of Mithra, or the sacred covenant between humanity and the divine. Through offerings, the practitioner renews this bond, reminding themselves of their place within the grand order of asha—the cosmic truth. The act of giving, whether through fire, water, or tangible items, mirrors the divine act of creation itself, where Ahura Mazda infused the universe with life and order. Offerings are thus a way for humans to participate in this continuous cycle of giving and receiving, a rhythm that echoes through the heart of existence.

One of the most ancient forms of offering is the Atash Nyash, the offering made to the sacred fire. In Zoroastrian temples and homes alike, the fire is seen as the earthly manifestation of the Light Divine, a symbol of Ahura Mazda's eternal presence. Practitioners offer sandalwood, frankincense, and ghee (clarified butter) into the fire, each material chosen for its purifying properties. As these substances burn, they release a fragrant smoke that carries the essence of the offering to the spiritual realm. The crackling flames, the rising smoke, and the warmth of the fire all become part of a dialogue between the devotee and the divine, a prayer that ascends with each wisp of scented air.

The symbolism of these materials is deeply woven into Zoroastrian cosmology. Sandalwood, known for its calming and purifying fragrance, represents the purification of thoughts, inviting clarity and serenity into the space. Frankincense is offered as a symbol of consecration, a substance that has been used for millennia to sanctify and make holy the spaces where it burns. Ghee, with its rich, nourishing qualities, symbolizes the nurturing aspect of the divine, sustaining the fire just as Ahura Mazda sustains the universe. When offered with intention, each of these materials becomes a vessel, carrying the prayers and desires of the practitioner into the realm of light.

Offerings are not limited to fire alone. The element of water, revered as Aban, also plays a significant role in Zoroastrian rites of offering. The Ab-Zohr ceremony, a water offering, is performed as a means of blessing the waters and invoking their purifying power. Practitioners pour water into a vessel, adding a few drops of consecrated Haoma (a sacred plant) or rose water to symbolize the infusion of divine life force. As they recite the verses of the Avesta, the water is envisioned as a channel for Ahura Mazda's blessings, purifying both the body and the spirit. This practice not only honors the sacredness of water but also recognizes its role as a life-giving force, aligning the practitioner with the flow of spiritual nourishment.

Another form of offering is the Dron, a simple yet profound ritual involving bread consecrated with ghee and prayer. The bread represents the sustenance provided by the earth, while the ghee symbolizes the essence of divine blessings. This offering, placed before the sacred fire or a shrine, serves as a reminder of the practitioner's dependence on divine grace for their physical and spiritual nourishment. The sharing of the Dron with others after the ritual becomes an act of communal blessing, where the sacred merges with the everyday, infusing even the simplest of meals with a sense of gratitude and reverence.

Offerings are also made through acts of service and charity, which are viewed as extensions of the physical offerings given in rituals. In Zoroastrianism, the spiritual value of an offering is not determined by its material worth but by the purity of the intention behind it. A simple meal shared with the less fortunate, a moment of kindness extended to a stranger, or the act of planting a tree—all of these are seen as offerings to Ahura Mazda. They embody the Zoroastrian principles of Spenta Mainyu, the progressive spirit, through which the practitioner becomes a conduit for divine light in the world. In this way, every act of generosity and service becomes a prayer in action, a living offering that resonates with the energy of asha.

The ritual of offering Haoma, a sacred plant revered in Zoroastrian tradition, is another key practice that connects the practitioner with the spiritual essence of life. The preparation of the Haoma drink involves the careful grinding of its leaves, accompanied by prayers that invoke the spirit of the plant. When consumed, Haoma is believed to confer divine wisdom and strength, aligning the soul with the virtues of truth and righteousness. The offering of Haoma is not just a physical act but a mystical experience, where the boundaries between the physical and spiritual worlds blur, allowing the practitioner to taste the essence of the divine directly.

Offerings of incense, known as Loban, also hold a special place in Zoroastrian worship. As the smoke of the incense spirals upward, it symbolizes the ascent of prayers and thoughts towards the heavens. The choice of incense can vary—each fragrance carries its own vibration, whether calming, invigorating, or purifying. During special ceremonies, the scent of Loban fills the air, transforming the space into a sacred vessel, echoing the ancient temples where such offerings were first made. The rising smoke is a visual representation of the soul's desire to reach higher realms, seeking connection with Ahura Mazda and the divine energies that shape the universe.

In the heart of all these practices lies the understanding that offerings are not about sacrifice or loss, but about the circulation of energy. When a practitioner offers something to the fire, to the water, or to another person, they are participating in the same cycle that keeps the stars in motion and the seasons turning. By giving, they create space within themselves to receive—more light, more wisdom, more connection to the divine. This flow of giving and receiving is an echo of the very breath of creation, a reminder that everything given with a pure heart returns a thousandfold in spiritual blessings.

The first step in making an offering is to create a space that reflects the purity and sanctity of the ritual. A small altar or sacred corner in the home can serve as a focal point for prayers and offerings. This space should be kept clean, free of distractions, and adorned with symbols that inspire the practitioner, such as a flame, a vessel of water, and sacred texts or images. Light a candle or the sacred fire before beginning, as the presence of the flame is a reminder of Ahura Mazda's eternal light. This preparatory act helps to center the mind and creates a tangible sense of entering a space that is dedicated to spiritual practice.

When choosing materials for an offering, it is important to consider their symbolic meaning and their resonance with the purpose of the ritual. Sandalwood and frankincense are often used in offerings to the fire, as their fragrances are believed to carry prayers into the spiritual realm. For water offerings, a few drops of rose water or Haoma can be added to symbolize purity and the essence of divine life. For those who wish to make food offerings, items such as fruit, bread, or ghee represent nourishment and the gifts of the earth, acknowledging the blessings that sustain physical life.

To begin the offering ritual, practitioners can recite the Ashem Vohu or the Yatha Ahu Vairyo, two powerful prayers that align the mind and heart with the principles of asha—truth and righteousness. These ancient verses act as an invocation, calling forth the presence of divine energies and inviting the blessings of Ahura Mazda into the space. As the words resonate in the air, the practitioner holds their offering—whether a piece of sandalwood, a cup of water, or a simple loaf of bread—focusing on the intention behind the act. This is the moment where the material meets the spiritual, where the mundane is elevated through the sincerity of the heart.

The act of offering to the fire, known as Atash Nyash, begins with gently placing the chosen material into the flames. As the wood or incense is consumed, the rising smoke is seen as a carrier of prayers, ascending to the higher realms. Practitioners are encouraged to visualize their intentions and prayers mingling with the smoke, rising toward Ahura Mazda. This visualization strengthens the connection between the physical and the spiritual, making the offering a vehicle for transformation. The flames become a living symbol of the practitioner's desire to be in harmony with the divine will, to let their thoughts and actions be purified in the heat of devotion.

For offerings made to water, the ritual follows a similar process of intention and invocation. As the practitioner pours the consecrated water into a natural body of water or a vessel kept at the altar, they recite prayers that bless the element and invite the purifying energies of Aban, the spirit of the waters. The water becomes a medium for carrying away negativity and invoking blessings, a mirror reflecting the desire for inner clarity. The ripples that spread as the water is poured symbolize the far-reaching effects of each act of devotion, echoing through the realms of spirit and matter.

The Dron ceremony, where bread is offered with ghee, can be performed with a similar sense of sacredness. Practitioners place the bread before the flame or shrine, anointing it with ghee as they recite verses that acknowledge the sustenance provided by Ahura Mazda. This simple act is an offering of gratitude, recognizing that all nourishment—physical and spiritual—flows from the divine source. After the ritual, the bread is shared with family or community members, turning the offering into an act of communal blessing. In this way, the divine presence invoked during the ritual extends beyond the individual, touching the lives of those around them.

To ensure that the energy of the offering is fully aligned with the practitioner's intention, it is important to reflect on the state of mind during the ritual. Zoroastrian teachings emphasize the purity of thoughts, words, and deeds, known as the Humat, Hukht, and Hvarsht. Practitioners are encouraged to enter the ritual with a clear mind and an open heart, setting aside any negativity or distractions. The act of offering should be performed with a spirit of generosity and humility, acknowledging that the material given is but a symbol of a deeper offering—the dedication of one's self to the path of light.

As the ritual concludes, it is customary to offer a closing prayer, thanking Ahura Mazda for the opportunity to connect with the divine through the act of offering. The practitioner may express gratitude for the guidance received and the blessings bestowed, sealing the ritual with a gesture of reverence such as a bow or a moment of silence. This final act helps to ground the energies raised during the ritual, ensuring that they are integrated into the practitioner's life and spiritual path.

The power of offerings extends beyond the ritual itself, shaping the practitioner's approach to life and relationships. Just as an offering is given freely and with intention, so too can acts of kindness and generosity be seen as offerings to the divine presence in all things. The daily interactions with others, the care given to nature, and the thoughts that shape one's inner world—all become opportunities to offer light to the universe. Through this practice, the line between the sacred and the mundane begins to blur, revealing the potential for each moment to become an offering in its own right.

In addition to these personal offerings, Zoroastrian communities often come together for communal rituals, where offerings are made collectively. These gatherings, whether during festivals like Nowruz or in remembrance of ancestors, strengthen the bonds between members of the community and the divine. The energy of shared intention amplifies the power of the offerings, creating a space where the presence of Ahura Mazda is felt as a collective experience. Such communal practices remind practitioners that their spiritual journey is not walked alone but is part of a larger tapestry of souls, each contributing their light to the greater whole.

By embracing the practice of offerings, practitioners are reminded of the flow of energy that sustains all of creation. Through these acts, they learn the art of giving and receiving, discovering that in each offering lies the potential to transform the self and the world. The flame consumes the wood, the water accepts the blessing, and the bread nourishes the spirit—each act a step closer to the divine, a thread weaving through the fabric of life. As they continue on their spiritual path, practitioners find that every offering, no matter how simple, is a testament to the ever-present light of Ahura Mazda, a light that guides, protects, and inspires.

Chapter 25
Rituals of Protection

Within the spiritual journey of Zoroastrianism, safeguarding the inner light and maintaining a connection to the divine presence of Ahura Mazda requires continuous protection. These protective rituals are essential for shielding the soul from negative influences, energies that might hinder the path toward purity and truth. Zoroastrian practices emphasize the importance of establishing a spiritual defense, creating a space where the energies of light can flourish without obstruction.

The act of protection begins with the understanding of vulnerability—recognizing that just as there is a divine light, there exist forces that seek to obscure it. These forces, whether external influences or internal doubts, are often represented within Zoroastrian cosmology as the shadows cast by Angra Mainyu, the Spirit of Destruction. It is against such disruptions that practitioners build their spiritual defenses, invoking the aid of Ahura Mazda, the Amesha Spentas, and the energy of sacred fire. These rituals not only protect but also purify, ensuring that the soul remains aligned with the path of asha, the cosmic order.

One of the central practices for daily protection is the recitation of Yasna prayers, specifically designed to fortify the mind and heart against negative thoughts and spiritual disturbances. The Ashem Vohu and Yatha Ahu Vairyo, as central prayers, are spoken with focused intent to invoke the presence of divine order and clarity. When reciting these prayers, practitioners visualize a bright flame surrounding them, acting as a spiritual armor that repels harmful energies. This mental imagery enhances the prayer's efficacy, creating a space within and around the practitioner that resonates with the purity of asha.

The Kushti ritual, which involves the sacred girdle worn by Zoroastrians, also plays a vital role in protection. Tying the Kushti around the waist while reciting specific mantras symbolizes a reaffirmation of the covenant with Ahura Mazda. This act serves as a reminder of the commitment to truth and righteousness, and it creates a spiritual boundary that shields the practitioner throughout the day. The motions of tying and untying the Kushti are not mere gestures; they are a continuous engagement with the divine, a weaving of one's life into the fabric of spiritual protection.

The power of fire as a guardian is central to Zoroastrian rituals of protection. Lighting a sacred flame in the home, even a small candle or lamp, is a daily reminder of the eternal light of Ahura Mazda. The presence of the fire acts as a purifier, burning away the traces of negativity that might cling to the physical or spiritual environment. In times of heightened need, such as during illness or distress, practitioners may perform the Atash Niyayesh—a prayer dedicated to the fire, asking for its protective and cleansing energies to surround the home and all those within it. The flame becomes a watchful sentinel, its flickering light a beacon of divine presence.

Water, too, holds a place in the rituals of protection. The use of ab-zor—water that has been blessed with prayers—can be sprinkled around the home, over thresholds, and even over oneself, forming a protective boundary that wards off malevolent energies. This practice is akin to creating a barrier that negative entities cannot cross, using the sanctity of water as a spiritual cleanser. The invocation of Ardvi Sura Anahita, the divine spirit of the waters, during this ritual further enhances its potency, calling forth her protection and guidance in maintaining purity within the environment.

Beyond the physical rituals, Zoroastrianism teaches that the mind itself is a fortress against negative influences. The practice of spenta mainyu, or the cultivation of positive thoughts, is a form of mental protection that shields against despair and temptation. Practitioners are encouraged to begin each day with affirmations of light and hope, using simple phrases like "I am surrounded by the light of Ahura Mazda" or "May the path of asha guide me." These thoughts, like the prayers, resonate beyond the individual, creating an aura of resilience that impacts the spiritual atmosphere of their surroundings.

One of the more communal aspects of protection involves coming together as a family or community to recite protective prayers, creating a collective shield of energy. Such gatherings, often held during festivals or in moments of communal concern, magnify the strength of each individual's efforts. The unity of voices chanting ancient words serves as a reminder that no one walks this path alone; each person's light contributes to the protection of the whole. In such moments, the boundaries between individual and collective dissolve, revealing a shared commitment to upholding the light amidst darkness.

The practices of protection in Zoroastrianism, while deeply rooted in tradition, also invite adaptability. In modern times, these rituals can be integrated into daily routines in ways that fit the practitioner's lifestyle, without losing their essence. A quiet moment in the morning to light a candle and recite a prayer before leaving the house, or a few drops of blessed water placed on the forehead before sleep—these adaptations retain the core purpose of aligning the individual with the energies of protection and light.

Each of these practices, whether simple or elaborate, forms part of a larger spiritual tapestry—a commitment to safeguarding the inner flame. By engaging with these protective rituals, practitioners cultivate a state of readiness, where the soul remains vigilant against the shadows, ever turning toward the light. Through them, they honor the teachings of Zoroaster, who spoke of a world where light and dark are in constant interplay, yet where the light, through steadfast practice and intention, always finds a way to prevail.

In the intricate fabric of Zoroastrian spiritual practice, protection extends beyond the individual to encompass the spaces we inhabit and the connections we share with others. It involves creating environments where the light can flourish, where the energies of Ahura Mazda resonate freely, undisturbed by forces that seek to disrupt the order of asha.

One of the most potent techniques in Zoroastrianism for maintaining a protected space is the ritual of consecrating the home through the Atash Dadgah, a home-based sacred fire. This ritual involves lighting a fire with great reverence, using elements such as sandalwood, frankincense, and dried herbs. The practitioner recites Atash Niyayesh—a prayer of devotion to the fire—while facing the flame, focusing on the intention of purification and protection. As the smoke rises, it is believed to carry the prayers into the spiritual realms, forming a shield that surrounds the dwelling. The act of tending to this fire regularly, even if only with a small flame, keeps the protective energies active, making the home a stronghold of divine presence.

To enhance the protective energy of a space, the Zoroastrian tradition also emphasizes the use of Nirang—sacred recitations and blessings that imbue objects or spaces with spiritual energy. For instance, practitioners can prepare ab-zor (blessed water) by reciting prayers over a bowl of water, such as the Ashem Vohu. This water is then used to anoint doorways, windows, and corners of the home, creating boundaries that discourage any negative entities from entering. As they sprinkle the water, practitioners may visualize a bright shield forming around their space, reflecting back any dark energies.

In environments where a physical flame is not possible, practitioners can invoke the light through visualizations. This involves sitting in a meditative state, closing the eyes, and imagining a sphere of glowing, white light expanding from the heart center, enveloping the entire body. Gradually, this light is extended beyond the self, until it encompasses the room and the home, creating a protective barrier that shields against unseen threats. This exercise, when performed daily, can be especially effective in places where negative energies feel particularly strong, such as during times of illness or emotional stress.

For those seeking to protect loved ones, Zoroastrian rituals also include the practice of Yazata invocations—calling upon the divine beings that serve Ahura Mazda for specific forms of protection. For instance, invoking Sraosha, the Yazata of divine obedience and protection, is common when seeking to guard a family member or child. The practitioner offers prayers and incense in the name of Sraosha, asking for his presence to watch over the vulnerable. Such rituals may be accompanied by the offering of myazda—food or flowers—placed beside a candle or incense, symbolizing the connection between the material and spiritual worlds.

Another layer of protection involves creating amulets or charms inscribed with holy words. The Yatha Ahu Vairyo, one of the most powerful mantras in Zoroastrianism, is often written or engraved on small metal plates or parchment, which are then kept close to the body or placed in homes. This mantra, believed to embody the essence of cosmic order, serves as a spiritual safeguard, redirecting negative energies away from the wearer. While traditionally these amulets might be blessed by a Mobed (priest), individuals can also create their own through sincere devotion and focused intent.

For practitioners living in areas prone to conflict or unrest, the Zoroastrian tradition offers the Baj ritual, which focuses on creating peace and stability in the immediate surroundings. This involves reciting specific prayers while facing the four cardinal directions, each time visualizing a barrier of light extending outwards. The recitation includes Khorshed Niyayesh (prayer to the Sun) and Meher Niyayesh (prayer to the Yazata of sunlight), which call upon the sun's energy as a symbol of clarity, strength, and unwavering light. This ritual is particularly potent when performed at dawn, aligning the practitioner's intentions with the rising sun, a symbol of renewal and divine oversight.

To cleanse spaces that have been exposed to negative events or conflicts, Zoroastrianism also recommends the use of sacred fire in the form of dhoop (incense) burning. Special blends of resins such as frankincense and myrrh, combined with dried herbs like sandalwood and rose petals, are burned in a vessel, and the smoke is carried through the home. As the smoke fills each corner, it is believed to drive away lingering shadows and restore the balance of light. This practice is often accompanied by the recitation of the Hormazd Yasht, a prayer that praises Ahura Mazda's supreme light and protection, invoking his presence to permeate every part of the dwelling.

In protecting one's environment, practitioners are also encouraged to remain mindful of the energy they bring into their own space. Zoroastrianism teaches that actions and thoughts leave imprints on the spiritual fabric of the home. Therefore, maintaining a space free of harsh words, negative thoughts, and conflicts is just as crucial as performing the rituals themselves. Daily acts of kindness, gratitude, and charity, even within the household, contribute to an atmosphere that naturally repels negativity.

Collective rituals for the community's protection can also be significant during times of societal unrest or natural challenges. Community gatherings around a temple fire, where multiple practitioners unite in reciting the Ahunavar or Ashem Vohu, generate a wave of positive energy that extends beyond the individual. These rituals serve as reminders that the strength of the light multiplies when shared, forming a vast network of spiritual protection that benefits all involved. For those unable to attend in person, joining in spirit by reciting the prayers at the same time from their homes can help build a collective shield.

Ultimately, these practices of protection, in their simplicity and depth, remind the practitioner that the light of Ahura Mazda is ever-present, ready to respond to those who seek it with sincerity. Through these methods, the individual learns to transform their home and surroundings into a sanctuary, where the divine presence is palpable, and where the shadows of doubt and fear find no foothold. As these rituals become a part of daily life, they weave an enduring connection between the material and spiritual realms, ensuring that the light within and around remains steadfast, unwavering in the face of adversity.

Chapter 26
Dream Interpretation

Dreams, within the Zoroastrian tradition, are not merely the echoes of the subconscious mind—they are considered windows to the spiritual realms, a bridge between the material world and the divine. For practitioners, dreams hold the potential to offer guidance, warnings, and blessings from Ahura Mazda and the Amesha Spentas, serving as a direct form of communication with the higher planes of existence.

Zoroastrianism regards the soul as a being that, during sleep, momentarily frees itself from the confines of the physical body, venturing into realms beyond the tangible. This nocturnal journey of the soul is a time when it may encounter spirits, both benevolent and malevolent, and receive impressions from the spiritual world. Dreams, therefore, are seen as records of these encounters, sometimes manifesting as clear visions and, at other times, appearing as veiled symbols that require interpretation.

Central to the Zoroastrian approach to dreams is the belief that certain visions are sent by Ahura Mazda to guide the practitioner on their spiritual journey. These dreams often carry themes of light, purity, and moral teachings, reflecting the principles of asha—the path of truth and righteousness. For instance, dreaming of a radiant flame or a brilliant sun is traditionally interpreted as a sign of spiritual favor and protection. Such dreams are believed to indicate that the practitioner is on a path aligned with divine will, encouraging them to continue their devotion and practice.

Conversely, dreams of darkness, confusion, or being pursued may signal a spiritual challenge or the presence of druj—

forces of deception and falsehood. These dreams are not to be feared but rather viewed as calls for increased vigilance in one's spiritual practices, such as more frequent recitations of protective prayers like the Yatha Ahu Vairyo or the Ashem Vohu. They serve as reminders of the ongoing struggle between light and shadow within the soul, urging the dreamer to seek clarity and strength through their connection to the divine.

The Zoroastrian tradition places particular emphasis on the appearance of the Yazatas—spiritual beings and divine emissaries—in dreams. When a practitioner dreams of a figure clad in light or hears a voice that speaks with authority and kindness, it is often interpreted as an encounter with a Yazata. For example, the presence of Mithra, the guardian of covenants and truth, might be revealed through dreams where themes of loyalty, oaths, or agreements are highlighted. Similarly, a vision of flowing waters or a serene landscape could signify the influence of Anahita, the Yazata of the waters, indicating a period of emotional healing or a need for purification.

Understanding the messages within dreams requires not only spiritual openness but also discernment, for not all dreams carry divine significance. Zoroastrian wisdom teaches that dreams arising from mundane thoughts, daily anxieties, or even indulgences should be distinguished from those that bear spiritual import. Practitioners are encouraged to cultivate a habit of reflection before sleep, offering a simple prayer such as the Hormazd Yasht, asking for clarity and true visions. This prayer invites Ahura Mazda to guide the soul through the nocturnal journey, steering it away from confusion and towards meaningful encounters.

To aid in this process, Zoroastrians have long practiced the art of keeping a dream journal. By recording their dreams upon waking, practitioners capture the vivid details that might fade with the morning light. These records become valuable tools for identifying recurring symbols and themes, allowing a pattern to emerge over time. The act of writing down dreams is itself seen as an offering to the divine, a way of demonstrating that the practitioner values the insights provided by the spiritual realm.

The interpretation of symbols within dreams is an intuitive process, often guided by the context of the dreamer's life and the specific teachings of Zoroastrianism. For instance, dreaming of fire can have multiple meanings depending on its context—while a steady, glowing flame might signify inner peace and divine presence, a fire that rages uncontrollably might symbolize unchecked passions or challenges to one's spiritual discipline. Similarly, a dream of crossing a river might represent a transition in the dreamer's spiritual journey, perhaps a time of testing and growth.

The dreamer's own spiritual state and recent practices can influence the nature of their dreams. For those who engage deeply with the recitation of mantras and prayers, dreams may become more vivid and direct, reflecting the strengthening of their connection to the spiritual world. This is particularly true during periods of fasting or spiritual retreats, when the mind is less burdened by physical concerns and more open to receiving divine messages. During these times, dreams can serve as a form of inner guidance, offering reassurance or pointing to areas in need of deeper attention.

Moreover, dreams that occur in the early hours of the morning, particularly during the time of the Ushahin Gah (dawn prayers), are considered especially potent in Zoroastrian belief. This time, when the first rays of sunlight begin to pierce the darkness, is viewed as a moment when the veil between the worlds is thinnest, allowing for clearer communication between the practitioner's soul and the higher realms. Dreams received during this sacred time are often seen as carrying messages directly from Ahura Mazda or the Amesha Spentas, offering insights that are meant to guide the practitioner through the day ahead.

Yet, even with all this knowledge, the interpretation of dreams is not meant to be rigid or deterministic. Zoroastrianism values the inner journey of each practitioner and encourages them to seek the meaning of their dreams through contemplation and dialogue with their own intuition. It is said that the light within each soul holds the answers, and that dreams are but reflections of the inner light striving to communicate with the conscious mind.

As the practitioner grows in their spiritual practice, they begin to understand the language of their own dreams, recognizing when a symbol is a personal message and when it is part of the larger, cosmic conversation between the worlds. Through this process, dreams become not only a tool for understanding one's path but a way of experiencing the living presence of the divine in the most intimate of realms—the inner world of the soul.

One of the foundational practices in interpreting dreams is the art of keeping a Nama Khvab, or dream journal. Upon waking, the practitioner is encouraged to write down every detail of their dream, even those that seem insignificant. This act of recording not only preserves the memory of the dream but also honors the messages that may have been imparted during the soul's nocturnal journey. The journal becomes a repository of symbols, emotions, and scenarios that can later be revisited and reflected upon for deeper understanding.

While writing, practitioners should note specific elements such as colors, numbers, and recurring symbols, as these often carry layers of spiritual meaning. For example, the presence of fire in a dream might signify purification or divine guidance, while water often represents the flow of emotions or the cleansing of the spirit. Each symbol has the potential to reflect the inner state of the dreamer or to highlight a spiritual lesson that needs attention. In this way, the journal serves as both a map and a mirror, guiding the dreamer through the landscape of their inner world.

After recording dreams, the next step is reflection and analysis. Practitioners are encouraged to meditate on the images and feelings evoked by their dreams, seeking insights that resonate with their current spiritual path. A method known as Khvab Tavili, or "dream contemplation," involves sitting quietly with the written record of a dream, breathing deeply, and inviting the mind to revisit the dreamscape. In this contemplative state, the dreamer allows the subconscious to reveal deeper layers of meaning, opening the door to intuitive understanding.

It is during these moments of stillness that the practitioner may recognize patterns or connections between their dreams and the teachings of the Zoroastrian faith. For instance, a recurring dream of crossing a bridge might be seen as a metaphor for the Chinvat Bridge, the crossing that each soul faces after death, symbolizing a time of transition or moral reckoning in the dreamer's life. Understanding these connections can help align one's waking actions with the messages received in dreams, turning spiritual insight into practical wisdom.

Rituals performed before sleep can enhance the clarity of dreams and open channels for spiritual communication. One such practice is the recitation of the Ahunavar (Yatha Ahu Vairyo) before bedtime, a sacred chant that aligns the practitioner's mind with the will of Ahura Mazda. By repeating this mantra, the dreamer sets an intention to receive guidance and protection during their sleep. It is believed that this invocation creates a shield of light around the soul, offering protection from deceptive influences and inviting true visions that align with the divine order.

Additionally, practitioners can prepare their sleeping environment to welcome spiritual insight. Placing a small vessel of water near the bed is a traditional practice that symbolizes the flow of divine wisdom and serves as a purifying presence in the dreamer's space. In the morning, this water can be used in a simple ritual of gratitude, pouring it onto the earth with a prayer of thanks for any messages received, thus closing the cycle of giving and receiving between the spiritual and physical realms.

Interpretation also benefits from community wisdom. Zoroastrian tradition holds that certain dreams, especially those that carry profound or unsettling messages, should be shared with a trusted spiritual guide or a member of the community with deep knowledge of the faith. This practice is rooted in the belief that guidance from others can provide clarity, especially when a dream's meaning is elusive or complex. Elders and Mobeds (priests) may offer insights that the dreamer alone might not perceive, viewing the dream through the lens of ancient teachings and spiritual understanding.

The guidance received through dreams is not always direct. Often, dreams use metaphors and symbols that reflect the dreamer's unique life and challenges. Therefore, while there are common interpretations for symbols like light, water, or fire within the Zoroastrian tradition, each practitioner is encouraged to develop a personal relationship with these symbols. A vision of a white bird, for example, might universally signify purity or a message from a higher realm, but for one individual, it could also represent a departed ancestor watching over them, or a call to embrace a specific spiritual path.

For practitioners seeking to deepen their dream practices, a specific ritual can be performed before sleep to request guidance on a particular question or challenge. Known as Mithra's Request—a nod to Mithra, the Yazata associated with oaths and truth—this ritual involves lighting a small flame before bedtime, focusing on the flame while silently stating one's question or desire for insight. The flame, as a manifestation of Ahura Mazda's light, serves as a conduit between the physical and spiritual worlds, carrying the practitioner's intention to the higher realms.

After stating the question, the practitioner extinguishes the flame with a breath, symbolizing the release of their request into the spiritual currents. Upon waking, they should immediately record their dream, paying close attention to any symbols or impressions that might relate to the question posed. This ritual is a way of engaging actively with the divine, trusting that the answer may come in the form of a vision, a symbol, or a feeling that guides them toward clarity.

It is also important to recognize the role of timing in dream interpretation. Zoroastrians believe that dreams occurring during certain times of the night carry different levels of significance. For example, dreams that come in the early morning hours, particularly before dawn, are considered to be the most spiritually potent, as they coincide with the time of Ushahin Gah, when the first light pierces the night and the veil between worlds is thinnest. Such dreams often carry messages meant to guide the dreamer through the challenges of the day or provide insight into their spiritual progress.

By integrating these practices into their nightly routines, practitioners can transform their sleep into a time of spiritual exploration and divine communion. Dreams become more than fleeting images—they become a sacred dialogue with the unseen, an opportunity to align more closely with the path of asha and the teachings of Ahura Mazda. The practical steps outlined here—journaling, contemplation, rituals, and community interpretation—provide a structured way to engage with this mystical aspect of Zoroastrian practice.

Yet, amidst these practices, it is crucial to remain humble and open-hearted, recognizing that not every dream holds profound significance. The Zoroastrian path encourages practitioners to balance reverence for the spiritual with a grounded approach to life. By doing so, the dreamer learns to discern which visions are true messages from the divine and which are simply the echoes of the mind's wanderings.

Dreams, like the flames that burn in Zoroastrian temples, illuminate but do not reveal all mysteries at once. Each night offers a chance to glimpse beyond the veil, to receive a spark of insight that, when nurtured, can grow into the fire of understanding. Through this nightly communion, practitioners draw closer to the eternal light of Ahura Mazda, weaving the wisdom of the night into the tapestry of their waking lives.

Chapter 27
Paths to Wisdom

The quest for wisdom is a cornerstone of the Zoroastrian spiritual journey, guiding practitioners beyond the mere acquisition of knowledge toward a deeper understanding of the mysteries that shape the cosmos and the inner self. Zoroastrian wisdom, however, is not simply about intellectual enlightenment—it is a holistic process, intertwining the teachings of the faith with the lived experience of the practitioner.

At the heart of this journey lies the concept of Chisti, which in Zoroastrian thought refers to divine wisdom or intuitive understanding that transcends ordinary reasoning. Chisti is considered a gift bestowed by Ahura Mazda, guiding the mind toward greater insight into the nature of reality. It is not something that can be grasped through logic alone but is revealed through spiritual practice and a life committed to the principles of asha, the cosmic order. Chisti is often described as a light that illuminates the hidden corners of the soul, revealing truths that were previously obscured.

To cultivate Chisti, Zoroastrians are encouraged to engage in khshnoom, a meditative practice that involves reflecting deeply upon the words of the Avesta—the sacred scriptures of Zoroastrianism. Khshnoom is not simply about recitation; it is an invitation to enter into the spiritual essence of the texts, allowing the meanings to unfold through layers of contemplation. The Avesta contains hymns, prayers, and stories that connect the believer with the timeless wisdom of Zaratustra, offering guidance on living in harmony with the divine law.

A common starting point in khshnoom is the study of the Gathas, the hymns attributed directly to Zaratustra. These hymns are considered the heart of Zoroastrian teachings, addressing profound themes such as the struggle between light and darkness, the nature of the divine, and the pursuit of righteous living. By meditating on these hymns, practitioners open themselves to the wisdom embedded within each verse, letting the teachings shape their understanding of the world and their place within it.

This process of study is not hurried. Instead, it is deliberate and reverent, with each line of the Gathas approached as a living expression of divine will. Practitioners often recite verses aloud during meditation, allowing the rhythmic cadence to resonate within their being. This vocalization is believed to attune the mind to the sacred vibrations of the words, creating a bridge between the earthly and the divine. As the recitations progress, insights may arise spontaneously, offering new perspectives on life's challenges or the nature of the self.

Beyond textual study, Zoroastrian practice emphasizes the importance of spenta mainyu, or a creative and progressive mentality. Spenta mainyu involves an openness to new ideas and a willingness to grow spiritually through reflection and the questioning of assumptions. This openness is not seen as a departure from tradition but as a vital part of the Zoroastrian path—an embrace of the evolving nature of wisdom. Just as Ahura Mazda is seen as a force of continuous creation, so too is the mind of the seeker encouraged to remain dynamic and receptive.

To practice spenta mainyu, Zoroastrians might engage in daily self-reflection, asking themselves questions that challenge their understanding and push them to consider new perspectives. For instance, a practitioner might meditate on the nature of asha and ask, "In what ways can I better align my actions with cosmic order?" or "How do my current beliefs reflect my understanding of Ahura Mazda's will?" This process of introspection is an opportunity to identify areas where growth is needed and to align more closely with the principles of truth and righteousness.

Another pathway to wisdom lies in direct communion with nature, which Zoroastrianism views as a reflection of the divine order. The natural world, in its cycles and rhythms, offers endless lessons for those who observe with patience and an open heart. Walking in nature or sitting by a flowing stream, practitioners might meditate on the interplay between the elements—earth, water, fire, and air—and the balance they represent. These meditations are a way to understand the principles of life and death, growth and decay, that mirror the larger spiritual truths of the universe.

Zoroastrian teachings also highlight the value of seeking wisdom through service to others. Engaging in acts of charity and community support, known as Humat, Hukhta, Hvarshta (Good Thoughts, Good Words, Good Deeds), is seen not only as a moral duty but as a path to deeper understanding. Through these actions, practitioners experience the interconnectedness of all beings and gain insights into the nature of compassion, humility, and selflessness. This service-based wisdom complements the contemplative practices, grounding spiritual insights in tangible actions that benefit the community and the world.

Furthermore, mentorship plays a crucial role in the transmission of wisdom within the Zoroastrian community. Traditionally, younger or less experienced practitioners are encouraged to learn from Mobeds (priests) or from elders who have spent their lives immersed in the teachings of the faith. This relationship is not one of rigid hierarchy but of mutual respect and shared learning. Elders share stories, teachings, and interpretations, while the seekers bring fresh questions and perspectives. This exchange ensures that wisdom remains a living, evolving tradition rather than a static doctrine.

In addition to studying sacred texts and engaging in reflection, practitioners are encouraged to cultivate wisdom through the observance of seasonal festivals like Nowruz and Mehregan. These festivals mark the cycles of nature and serve as reminders of the eternal truths embedded within the changing seasons. During these times, community gatherings provide opportunities to discuss spiritual topics, share experiences, and deepen collective understanding. The act of celebrating together reinforces the bonds between individuals and the cosmic rhythms, offering a communal space for the flowering of wisdom.

Dreams, too, play a role in guiding the seeker toward wisdom. As discussed in the previous chapter, dreams can serve as a medium through which Ahura Mazda communicates directly with the soul, offering insights that might not be accessible in waking life. Practitioners learn to trust these nocturnal messages, weaving them into their understanding of themselves and their spiritual journey. A dream might suggest a new direction in one's studies or reveal a hidden truth about a personal challenge, becoming a beacon of light in moments of uncertainty.

Yet, amidst these practices, Zoroastrianism teaches that true wisdom is not a destination but a journey—an ever-unfolding path toward greater alignment with the divine. The seeker of wisdom learns to hold humility at the core of their quest, recognizing that the mysteries of creation are vast and that each insight is but a glimpse of the whole. This humility ensures that the wisdom attained does not lead to arrogance but to a deeper reverence for the divine order and the endless journey toward enlightenment.

In this way, the Zoroastrian path to wisdom becomes a dance between study and experience, contemplation and action, solitude and community. It is a path that invites each practitioner to become a living vessel of light, reflecting the wisdom of Ahura Mazda through their thoughts, words, and deeds. As they walk this path, they carry with them the understanding that every moment, every interaction, holds the potential to reveal another facet of the divine. Thus, the journey of seeking wisdom is, in truth, a journey of embracing the light that lies both within and beyond, leading ever closer to the eternal flame of understanding.

The pursuit of wisdom within Zoroastrianism deepens as one moves from the conceptual understanding of divine truths to their practical application in daily life.

Central to this process is the practice of reflective reading, known in the Zoroastrian tradition as muraqabah, which involves a slow and deliberate study of the sacred texts. Rather than reading to gather information, muraqabah invites the practitioner to engage deeply with the words, pondering their meanings and allowing them to resonate within the soul. For example, when reading a passage from the Yasna—the liturgical core of the Avesta—one might pause to consider how the divine principles described reflect in the natural world, in the self, and in the patterns of daily life.

During muraqabah, practitioners are encouraged to keep a spiritual journal, recording their reflections and any intuitive insights that arise during their studies. This practice helps in identifying recurring themes or divine messages that might be guiding the practitioner in a particular direction. For instance, if the concept of asha (truth and order) frequently emerges in one's reflections, it may indicate a call to focus on aligning one's actions more closely with this principle. This journaling becomes a repository of personal wisdom, a testament to the ongoing dialogue between the individual and the divine.

Meditative visualization, introduced in earlier chapters, also plays a key role in embodying wisdom. A particularly powerful technique involves visualizing oneself surrounded by the light of Ahura Mazda, with each breath drawing this light deeper into the heart. In these moments, the practitioner imagines the light filling the mind, clearing away confusion and revealing hidden truths. This light is seen not just as an abstract concept but as a living presence, guiding decisions and fostering clarity. As this practice deepens, it can become a source of intuitive knowledge that supports the practitioner in navigating life's complexities.

Wisdom in Zoroastrian practice is not confined to solitary contemplation; it flourishes through sohbat, the act of gathering in community to discuss spiritual insights. Zoroastrian communities often hold study circles where practitioners come together to reflect on passages from the Gathas or to discuss the meanings of seasonal rituals like Nowruz and Mehregan. These discussions provide a space where collective wisdom emerges, with each participant offering their unique perspective, enriching the understanding of all. Through sohbat, individuals learn the art of active listening and the humility to consider other viewpoints as facets of the same divine truth.

In addition to community gatherings, mentorship remains a critical pathway for deepening one's wisdom. Practitioners might seek the guidance of a Mobed, learning not only through direct instruction but also through the observation of their mentor's conduct and devotion. This relationship is often seen as a sacred bond, where the Mobed serves as a living example of Zoroastrian principles in action. By witnessing the way a mentor navigates challenges, maintains their connection to the divine, and expresses compassion, the seeker gains insights that cannot be found in books alone.

To further integrate wisdom into daily life, Zoroastrian teachings emphasize the cultivation of Frashokereti—the renewal of the world through positive thoughts, words, and deeds. Practitioners are encouraged to see each moment as an opportunity to contribute to the cosmic battle between light and darkness. For example, a simple act of kindness to a stranger, or the choice to speak truthfully even when difficult, becomes a way to manifest asha in the world. These acts, though small, are believed to ripple outward, contributing to the greater restoration of balance in the universe.

Practitioners are also guided to perform daily nirang, or short invocations, to maintain their spiritual focus throughout the day. These invocations, drawn from the Avesta, serve as reminders of divine principles and help ground the mind amidst the distractions of worldly life. A common invocation might be the recitation of Ashem Vohu, which speaks of the goodness that arises from righteousness. By repeating such phrases with mindfulness, the practitioner keeps their thoughts aligned with the higher truths, ensuring that wisdom informs their interactions and decisions.

The act of service, known as keshash, is another method of applying wisdom in a tangible way. Zoroastrianism teaches that serving others with a pure heart not only aids those in need but also refines the spirit of the giver. This service might take the form of assisting in community rituals, offering help to those facing hardship, or even taking care of the natural world through acts of environmental stewardship. Each of these acts is seen as a direct manifestation of the divine light within the individual, a living expression of Spenta Mainyu—the spirit of beneficence that opposes chaos and destruction.

Rituals that mark significant life events, such as Navjote (the initiation ceremony) or marriage, also serve as moments of profound reflection and the integration of wisdom. During these ceremonies, the community comes together to celebrate and affirm the commitments made by the individual. These rituals are steeped in symbolism, with each action reminding the participant of their role within the larger cosmic order. For example, the recitation of the Yatha Ahu Vairyo during Navjote symbolizes the alignment of one's will with the will of the divine, a pledge to walk the path of wisdom throughout life.

Another profound practice is seeking wisdom through nature, often referred to as Yazata contemplation. Practitioners immerse themselves in the elements—standing by a river, walking in the mountains, or simply sitting in the presence of fire. Each element is seen as a reflection of Ahura Mazda's creative power, and by meditating in such settings, the practitioner tunes into the rhythm of creation itself. In the presence of a flowing river, one might meditate on the nature of change and the constancy of life's flow, drawing lessons about adaptability and resilience.

Dream interpretation continues to be a valuable tool for integrating wisdom. Practitioners are taught to approach their dreams as reflections of their inner state, offering glimpses into their subconscious and their spiritual journey. Upon waking, the details of a dream are recorded and then meditated upon, seeking patterns or symbols that relate to their current spiritual path. For instance, a dream of light breaking through clouds might be seen as a sign of forthcoming clarity or a deeper understanding of a particular struggle. Through such practices, the line between waking wisdom and the wisdom of the dream world becomes more fluid.

Lastly, hamazoori, or the unity of purpose, emphasizes the importance of aligning one's life with the greater mission of spreading light and truth in the world. Zoroastrianism teaches that each person's journey toward wisdom is not isolated but interconnected with the journeys of others. Practitioners are encouraged to find ways to share their insights, whether through teaching, writing, or simply embodying the principles they have internalized. By doing so, they contribute to a collective awakening, where the wisdom of the few can inspire the many.

As the seeker moves through these practices, wisdom is no longer perceived as an abstract goal but as a lived reality, shaping every aspect of their existence. It is a process that requires patience, perseverance, and a deep trust in the guidance of Ahura Mazda. Each step taken with sincerity—whether in meditation, study, or service—adds another layer to the tapestry of understanding. This path to wisdom is unending, a journey that grows richer with each insight gained, each truth uncovered, and each moment lived in alignment with the divine.

Epilogue

Upon reaching the end of this journey, the shadows seem more distant, and the clarity of truth becomes brighter. What you found here is not an endpoint but a new beginning, a seed planted deep within that will continue to grow, reflecting the light of Ahura Mazda in each moment of your existence. The practices, rituals, and reflections presented have polished the purest parts of you, revealing a simple yet powerful truth: light and darkness are not distant entities but elements present throughout your life. The way you choose to nourish the light or stray from it shapes not only the world around you but the entire universe.

This book has served as a guide to rediscover your role as a guardian of asha, the cosmic principle that governs all things. This order is not an external imposition but a manifestation of your own essence. Each act of kindness, each pure thought, each gesture of compassion becomes an affirmation of the cosmic order, a beacon that lights your path and those around you. Just as the sacred fire is never extinguished in temples, you now perceive that within you exists a flame that burns, immortal and constant, resisting the temptations of darkness.

The teachings of Zoroaster, the practices of purification, and the understanding of sacred symbols are not fragments of a lost past but part of a living heritage. By applying this knowledge, you participate in an ancient tradition, a current of faith and transformation that transcends time and space. The asha you discovered throughout these pages should not be viewed as something distant or idealized; it lives in each of your gestures, in each of your thoughts, in the love and justice you choose to express.

This is not the end of your search; on the contrary, it is an invitation to continue treading the path of light, ever more firm, ever more aware. May you always remember the essential role of light—of your light—in maintaining the universe's balance and harmony. As you close the book, know that each small act of kindness and every honest choice strengthens the universal light, guiding humanity closer to the ideal of a renewed world, a reality where peace and order manifest in their fullness.

This is the beginning of a new journey, where each day becomes an invitation to purity, self-knowledge, and love. May your life, like the eternal fire of the temples, be a constant celebration of the divine light, a testament that truth and purity are eternal.